MODERN MOM'S BREASTFEEDING GUIDE

ALEXANDRA VEAL

Modern Mom's Breastfeeding Guide

by Alexandra Veal

CONTENTS

INTRODUCTION

B reastfeeding is a journey that binds all of us in its universality yet remains unique in its experience for every mother and child. It's a natural process, but that doesn't mean it comes naturally to everyone. It's filled with moments of joy, love, and sometimes, unexpected challenges that result in feelings that are hard to handle. As a mother of three, each of my breastfeeding experiences has taught me something new about this intricate dance between mother and baby. I've navigated through everything from mastitis and engorgement to hormonal issues, rashes and dairy sensitivities along with breastmilk storage, planning for absences and going back to work. While this is a book about breastfeeding, there will be information here about how newborn babies are affected by breast milk and some special side notes that new moms can benefit from. Each of my children brought their own peculiarities, challenges and memories to our breastfeeding journey.

This book is crafted with you in mind—whether you're a first-time mother feeling overwhelmed by the plethora of feeding options or you're a seasoned parent looking for new insights or reassurance. It's designed to be a warm, supportive guide that walks you through various aspects of breastfeeding—from mastering the latch in the early days in the hospital, to balancing work and pumping, to dealing with common feeding issues. It doesn't stop there; it also explores the healing properties of breastmilk for both baby and skincare, among other uses. In addition, you will find tips along the way for conquering breastfeeding from newborn life through month 12 and beyond.

My aim is to provide a balanced perspective, backed by the latest research and enriched with expert opinions, to ensure you have reliable and practical information at your fingertips. I've also included personal stories and those of other mothers to offer you a spectrum of experiences. This is not just a manual; it's a companion on your breastfeeding journey made by moms for moms just like you.

As we explore together, you'll find that this book is structured to flow from the basics of breastfeeding and its benefits, like the invaluable colostrum in the early days, to more advanced topics such as combining breastfeeding with bottle-feeding, managing supply issues and balancing a full time job with your breastfeeding and pumping needs. Lastly, but certainly not least important, we will discuss postpartum self-love and feature different ways to make sure you are able to maintain mental sanity through the breastfeeding journey.

I encourage you to use this book not just as a read-through guide but as a resource to come back to. Each chapter stands alone, allowing you to easily refer back to topics as needed. Whether you're looking for tips on pumping at work or need reassurance during those tough nights of cluster feeding, this guide is here to support you.

Every chapter of this book holds the understanding and encouragement of someone who's been right where you are now. I'm here with you, cheering you on as you navigate the highs and lows of breastfeeding alongside over 2 billion other mothers in the world. Together, let's nurture confidence in your breastfeeding journey, embracing each moment with knowledge, compassion, and care.

Welcome to your modern breastfeeding guide, for moms and by moms just like you—where every question is valid, and every challenge has a solution. You are ready! Here we go!

CHAPTER ONE

PREPARING FOR BREASTFEEDING SUCCESS

In the first moments after your baby arrives in this world, the connection you establish sets a profound foundation for your breastfeeding experience. Many mothers look forward to this phase with a mix of excitement and nervousness, wondering how they will fare when the time comes to nourish their newborn. It's a natural concern, and rightly so, because breastfeeding, while natural, isn't always easy. It requires a great deal of patience and commitment paired with a spirit of flexibility and compassion.

As you navigate the early stages of breastfeeding, remember why this journey is special. Breastfeeding gives your child a fantastic start in life, offering the perfect blend of nutrients, antibodies, and enzymes for healthy growth. It guards against infections, allergies, and chronic conditions such as obesity and diabetes. When we discuss latch, contact, and other factors, know that a good latch ensures efficient feeding and less discomfort for you, while skin-to-skin contact encourages bonding and milk production.

Any amount of breastmilk is beneficial, so if you produce only a little or need to supplement with formula later, every drop of breastmilk is a victory. Your breastfeeding experience is unique and valuable. Don't compare yourself to others; your success lies in nourishing your baby, whatever form that takes. Below is a diagram illustrating the benefits of breastmilk compared to formula. Remember, every step on this journey is significant.

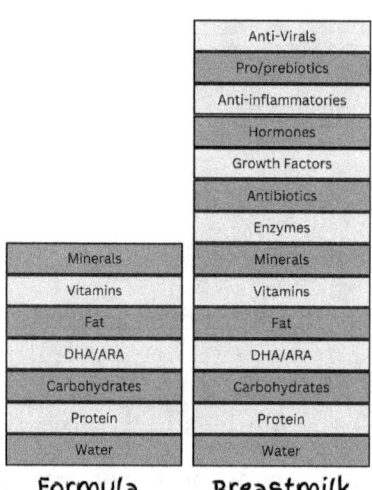

Remember, your first interactions with your baby lay the groundwork for your breastfeeding journey. Let's start right at the beginning—the magical first hour after your baby's birth. This golden hour is an opportunity to bond deeply and start your breastfeeding experience on a positive note. We'll delve into maximizing skin-to-skin contact, a simple yet powerful practice that significantly benefits both you and your baby.

1.1 The First Hour After Birth: Maximizing Skin-to-Skin Contact

The moment your baby is born, a new chapter in your life begins. Amid the relief and joy, there's a beautiful, instinctual practice that can profoundly impact both your and your baby's well-being: skin-to-skin contact. Placing your newborn against your skin isn't just a tender act of love; it's a powerful initiation into the world outside the womb that offers incredible benefits.

Importance of Immediate Contact

From the minute your baby is placed on your chest, the benefits begin to unfold. Skin-to-skin contact is not just about physical closeness; it facilitates a deep emotional bond that signals safety and comfort to your newborn. This contact helps in significantly reducing stress for both of you. Studies have shown that babies who are held skin-to-skin with their mothers exhibit lower stress indicators compared to those who are swaddled or placed in cribs immediately after birth. This calming effect also encourages the release of oxytocin in your body, often referred to as the 'love hormone,' which is crucial for affection and relaxation, and plays a significant role in the milk ejection reflex.

Birth and Breastfeeding

I want you to know that it is not going to hurt your breastfeeding journey if your contact with the baby is delayed. All three of my children were born via c-section and did not get immediate contact with me. However, we have had three very successful breastfeeding journeys, so give your-self some grace. Sometimes those timelines are out of your control. The most important thing is for you and your baby to be taken care of and to start your breastfeeding experience as soon as possible, within reason.

Initiating Breastfeeding

During these first skin-to-skin moments, your baby's innate feeding instincts kick in. Babies naturally start to 'root' or search for the breast when placed on their mother's chest, a fascinating process often culmi-nating in a baby latching on by themselves. This self-latching not only promotes a sense of achievement and connection for you both but also kick starts your breastfeeding effectively. Allowing your baby to find your breast at their own pace can lead to a better latch, which is essential for effective breastfeeding. This natural progression into breastfeeding helps in establishing a good milk supply right from the start. If your baby does not 'root' and latch on their own, do not panic. None of mine were able to latch on through the "rooting" method. There are multiple holds for breastfeeding that we will get to later, but to help my three latch I got in an upright sitting position in the hospital bed and held their head in my hand with their body resting on my forearm. With my other hand, using the thumb and pointer finger I 'pinched' the areola and nipple area and helped them get it into their mouth. For a good latch most of the areola should be in the baby's mouth. The goal is for the nipple to be toward the roof of the mouth with more of the bottom of the areola in their mouth than the top. I used this method for about the first 48 hours to get them a quality latch and to know what that quality latch looks and feels like. Also, make sure their whole body is facing you, not just their head. Below is a depiction of a high quality latch.

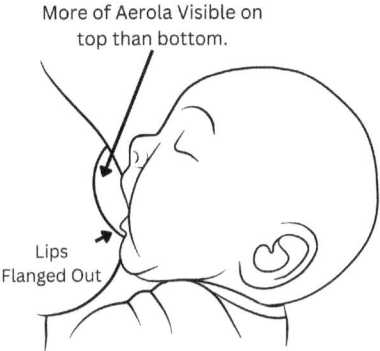

Thermal Regulation

Beyond emotional benefits, skin-to-skin contact has practical health implications. Your body acts like a natural incubator. Maintaining your baby's body temperature can be a challenge right after birth, as babies lose heat rapidly. Your body warmth helps regulate your newborn's temperature more effectively than most warming devices used in maternity wards. This thermal regulation is essential for newborns to maintain body energy and focus on growth and development. As your newborn grows, studies indicate that SIDS risk is reduced when the baby spends skin to skin time with their mother.

Stabilizing Baby's Vital Signs

The stability of your baby's vital signs is another compelling reason to practice immediate skin-to-skin contact. This simple act helps stabilize the baby's heart rate and breathing pattern, aligning them more closely with physiological norms. Babies who are held close in the first hour after birth often have a more regular heartbeat and a steadier breathing rate than those who are not. This stabilization is pivotal in the early adaptation phase outside the womb and can contribute significantly to the overall health of your newborn.

1.2 Understanding Colostrum: Your Baby's First Superfood

In the initial days following birth, your baby will be nourished by colostrum, often hailed as the first 'superfood' your newborn will ingest. This early milk, rich yet surprisingly low in fat, is packed with high levels of proteins and antibodies crucial for your baby's health. Colostrum serves as a potent natural vaccine, as it is densely loaded with immunoglobulin A (IgA), which is vital for protecting your baby's nascent immune system. IgA coats the lining of your baby's immature intestines, helping to fend off pathogens and allergens by forming a protective seal. This natural barrier is essential, considering that your baby's immune system is still developing and is initially quite vulnerable to infections.

The protein component in colostrum is significantly higher than in mature breast milk, which supports the initial growth spurts and aids in the development of vital organs and systems. Its low fat content is perfectly designed for a newborn's digestion, which is still gearing up for more complex baby foods down the line. This thoughtful composition not only facilitates easier digestion but also ensures that all the energy is directed towards essential developmental processes and not merely digesting the food itself.

Now, let's discuss the volume of colostrum your body produces. It's common for new mothers to worry about the seemingly small amount that they can express, often mistaking it for insufficient feeding volume. However, it's important to understand that a newborn's stomach is minuscule—about the size of a cherry on the first day, growing to about the size of a walnut by the third day. Thus, the small quantity of colostrum, which ranges from a few milliliters during the first feedings, is actually just right for your baby's limited stomach capacity. This perfectly portioned meal ensures that your baby gets all the necessary nutrients without over-whelming their tiny digestive system. Just know that your body produces and supplies the colostrum that your baby needs.

Feeding frequency during these initial days is another area where new insights can be really helpful. Colostrum is digested quicker than mature milk, so it's normal for your newborn to need frequent feedings—typically every one to three hours. This might seem daunting, but frequent feed-ings help stimulate your milk production and keep your baby adequately nourished. Also, each feeding session doesn't just fill your baby's belly but also helps cement the bonding process, stabilizes their heart rate, temper-ature, and breathing, and calms both of you as your body is experiencing hormonal changes as well as recovering from birth.

The long-term benefits of colostrum extend far beyond these early days. It sets up a foundation for a healthier life, with fewer allergies and illnesses. The antibodies and prebiotics contained in colostrum help develop a ro-bust digestive system, which is crucial as this is where much of the immune system is actually located. Moreover, the introduction of colostrum early in life is linked to a reduced risk of chronic conditions such as obesity and diabetes later in life. This magical first milk does more than just feed; it also builds, protects, and strengthens your baby in numerous unseen yet significant ways.

While it is not required, it is possible to express colostrum starting at about the 37-week mark. Some women hand express small amounts of colostrum before birth to use when needed. While I did not do this with any of my children, I know many moms that have. If you choose to express colostrum before birth, save it in small vials. Many moms indicate that it is easier to hand express colostrum rather than use a pump due to the thicker consistency. If you have colostrum stored prior to birth, many choose to take it to the hospital to ensure that your baby gets your colostrum instead of formula if, for some reason, you are unable to nurse your baby soon after birth. Stored colostrum can also be used later to help babies recover from illnesses that arise in the first year.

1.3 Decoding Baby's Hunger Cues and Feeding on Demand

When you first hold your newborn, the world seems to pause. It is at this time when you start noticing different actions of your baby. One of the first skills you'll develop is recognizing when your little one is hungry. This isn't just about ensuring they're fed; it's about building a responsive feeding relationship that nurtures their growth and your bond. Hunger cues in newborns can be subtle, and catching these early signs is key to a smooth breastfeeding experience and avoiding the agitation of a hungry baby.

The four most common ways a newborn communicates hunger includes:

- Waking up from sleep (strange, I know): When your baby sleeps, their body is using the fuel you are giving them, so oftentimes, they begin waking when their body needs more fuel.

- Making sucking motions with their mouth: While it may be cute and appear like they are dreaming about eating, most of the time, if your baby is making sucking motions, they are ready to nurse.

- Turning their head from side to side: the first time my second born did this, I felt like he was confused about where to find the breast, but turns out that it is the beginning of hunger and a minimal effort on their part to locate the next meal.

- Opening the mouth when close to skin: If your baby opens their mouth when they get close to you, they are probably hungry. This rooting activity is one of the best signs that your baby will eat.

These indications individually or any combination of them can be a signal that it is time to offer your baby something to eat. If these cues are missed and the baby starts crying and fussing, they may become too agitated to develop a good latch. This agitation isn't just hard on your baby; it can be stressful for you too and can make the feeding process feel more like a battle than a bonding activity. That's why recognizing and responding to early hunger signs is so important. Give yourself some grace. You will miss hunger cues and your baby will likely cry and kick their legs in frustration, but over time you will learn when your baby needs to eat.

Responsive feeding, or feeding on demand, plays a pivotal role in establishing a healthy milk supply that adapts to your baby's growing needs. Unlike strict feeding schedules, responsive feeding encourages you to offer the breast whenever your baby shows signs of hunger. This approach can feel daunting at first—wondering if you're feeding too little or too much. However, it's beneficial because it tailors to the natural variability in babies' appetites, which can fluctuate due to growth spurts or slight day-to-day changes in their development. By feeding on demand, you're essentially trusting in your baby's ability to regulate their intake according to their body's needs, which supports their metabolic health and helps in establishing an adequate milk supply as your body adjusts to produce milk based on the frequency and intensity of feeding. Feeding on demand is thus not just a method but a philosophy of responding to your baby with attention and care that extends beyond the breastfeeding period into other areas of their growth and development.

It is during the time when your milk comes in that you can make a significant impact on your milk production. There are various schools of thought on how to respond when your milk comes in. For some, they want to get regulated to just meet their baby's needs and not create any additional milk for storage. In my case, I knew I only had a short period of time to be home and I would need a 'stash' of milk in the freezer. Additionally, if you have a forceful letdown, you may find that you need to pump some milk BEFORE your baby can nurse. My first son got choked on my letdown every time I tried to nurse him, so for the first several weeks, I would pump through my letdown and then allow him to nurse. As they grow, they are more capable of dealing with the amount of milk from your letdown, but initially, it may be beneficial to pump a little before nursing. Some will say that pumping and nursing just encourages your body to make more milk, and it does, but for me, that was ok.

During the first few weeks of each of my children's lives I was able to put over 500 ounces of milk in the freezer and that gave me a great deal of relief for when I knew I would be going back to work. We will talk more about pumping and how to maintain the use of breastmilk if you have to return to work. For now, let's keep going.

1.4 Setting Up a Breastfeeding-Friendly Environment at Home

Creating a nurturing environment for breastfeeding isn't just about making physical adjustments; it's about cultivating a space where you feel supported, relaxed, and free from stress. It's where both you and your baby will spend a lot of time, so it's worth considering how to make this area as comfortable and functional as possible.

It is much easier to set up a special place with the first child. Once you get more than one, it is a bit more difficult to get solitude for breastfeeding. It would be phenomenal to have a space that is only used when breastfeeding and if you can set up that space with the items you need close, some calming music and a comfy chair, I am all for it. In our home, typically breastfeeding occurred wherever we were, most of the time in the living area. One thing I will recommend is getting you a few portable breastfeeding supply kits. I used a cleaning tote and put all the things you may need in it. That includes nipple shield, vitamin D drops, nipple cream, milk pads, and anything else that makes your breastfeeding session easier. Oddly enough, a cleaning caddy works great for this. They do also make cute ones for babies, but I like the cleaning caddy because it is heavy duty and can be repurposed later.

Again, do not put too much pressure on yourself to only breastfeed where you set up your 'spot'. I did this with my first son, and it caused me a considerable amount of undue stress. The most important thing is that you are comfortable, and your baby can get a good latch. Aside from that, the rest is fluff.

1.5 Essential Gear for Breastfeeding Moms

When it comes to breastfeeding, having the right gear can make a world of difference. It's not just about making the process easier—though that's certainly a huge benefit—it's also about ensuring you can do what you need to do efficiently and effectively. Let's delve into some essential items that I found invaluable during my breastfeeding experience, and that you might find beneficial too.

Breastfeeding Pillows

One of the first items I recommend is a good breastfeeding pillow. These aren't just your average pillows; they're designed to support your baby in the optimal position for breastfeeding, which can significantly reduce the strain on your arms, neck, and back. Trust me, when you're feeding multiple times a day (and night), this becomes incredibly important! There are several styles to choose from depending on your body shape and preferred feeding positions. For instance, the wrap-around pillows provide great all-around support, especially useful in the early days when you're still finding your feet while breastfeeding. On the other hand, compact pillows are fantastic for traveling or for those who don't have much space at home. They help elevate your baby to the right height, promoting a good latch, and can be a game changer in preventing discomfort during those long feeding sessions. My pillow was much more useful in weeks 1-6 as I was healing from a c-section and needed that extra support. I know some moms that use them for months, but for me, once the baby got stronger, we could nurse proficiently without the pillow. At that time, we used the nursing pillow to prop up the baby to a sitting position. After those uses, it became somewhat less of a tool we used daily.

Nursing Attire

Next, let's talk about what to wear. Nursing attire has come a long way in terms of style and functionality. Gone are the days of limited options; now, you can choose from various bras, tops, and dresses that look good and make breastfeeding that much easier. Nursing bras are a must—they provide essential support without underwires, which can be uncomfortable and may clog milk ducts. Look for bras with easy-to-open clasps that you can manage one-handed (because you'll often be holding your baby in the other arm!). Nursing tops and dresses typically feature discreet panels or layers that allow for easy access without sacrificing your privacy or sense of style. Whether you're at home or out and about, these garments can make you feel more comfortable and confident while breastfeeding. I did not require a nursing bra in the hospital, as my milk did not come in for a few days. In the hospital I used a top that had the double panel and would allow for easy access. I would recommend getting both the nursing bra and nursing tank. In early weeks, I lived in the nursing tank while I was able to transition to the nursing bra as I went back to work. The nursing bra is also great for pumping and access when you need to pump at work later in your journey.

Breast Pads and Nipple Cream

Then there are breast pads and nipple cream—small but mighty tools in your breastfeeding arsenal. Even if you're blessed with a relatively easy breastfeeding experience, leaks can and do happen. Breast pads are a simple solution. They tuck into your bra, keeping you dry and comfortable. You can choose between disposable and reusable options depending on your preference. As for nipple cream, it can be a lifesaver, especially in the first few weeks when your nipples may become sore as they adjust to frequent feeding. Look for creams that are safe for your baby so that you don't have to wash it off before feeding. These creams can help soothe and heal the skin, making breastfeeding more comfortable for you. Keep these items in multiple locations around the home, car, office or other places you frequent.

Breast Pump and Storage Containers

Finally, even if you plan to exclusively breastfeed, a breast pump can give you more flexibility and freedom. There are times when you might need to be away from your baby, or you may want to build up a store of milk for emergencies. That's where a good breast pump comes in. There are several types on the market, from manual to electric, portable to hospital grade. Your choice will depend on how often you plan to use it and your specific needs. Along with the pump, you'll need storage containers for the milk you express. These containers should be sterile and made from safe, durable materials that can be used in the fridge or freezer. Proper storage is crucial to ensure that the milk remains safe and retains its nutritional quality when your baby needs it.

With my first two sons, I pumped milk and immediately bagged it and placed it in the freezer. With my last child, I have used a pitcher method. I keep a 32 oz glass pitcher in the refrigerator and add milk to it until it is full then bag it, making sure I bag every three days. With this method, if the baby needs to bottle-feed, the milk is recent and available, also saving storage bags from being wasted. If you can breastfeed and do not have to be away from the baby for extended periods of time, you may not need an extensive storage plan. If you have to return to work, you can put the pitcher method or freezer method into practice. We will talk more about some of those options later.

Each of these items, from pillows to pumps, plays a role in simplifying the breastfeeding process, making it less of a strain. As with all aspects of parenting, what works best can vary widely from one person to another. It's all about finding what works for you and your baby, creating a breast-feeding experience that is as smooth and loving as possible. Remember, each feeding is not just about nourishment; it's a moment of connection, a quiet bond that you are building with your child to ensure safety and security.

CHAPTER TWO

MASTERING THE ART OF LATCHING

G etting the perfect latch might just be the most talked-about aspect of breastfeeding. Think of it as the key to a treasure chest; when it's right, it unlocks all the nourishing goodness of breastfeeding. But when it's off, it can be a source of pain and frustration. I remember those early days with my firstborn, feeling like we were both trying to solve a complex puzzle. It was those challenges that taught me the importance of mastering the art of latching. In this chapter, we'll explore just how you can achieve that perfect latch and how latching changes as your baby grows.

2.1 The Anatomy of a Good Latch

Visual Guides

Imagine you're drawing a small circle, the circle represents the areola, and the tiny dot in its center is the nipple. For a good latch, your baby's mouth should cover a substantial portion of the areola, not just the nipple.

This technique ensures that the milk ducts located under the areola are properly compressed during feeding, facilitating a good milk flow.

Signs of a Good Latch

How do you know if the latch is just right? There are a few telltale signs that indicate your baby is latched on effectively. First, you should see more of the areola above your baby's upper lip than below their lower lip. You might also hear a soft, rhythmic swallowing sound as your baby feeds, which is music to any breastfeeding mom's ears, signaling that your baby is getting plenty of milk. Additionally, your baby's lips should be turned outward, not tucked in, resembling the petals of a blooming flower. This "flanged" lip position helps create a tight seal to efficiently extract milk. A note here about the flanged lips. With all of my kids, I have occasionally had to help them get their lips in the right position. You can take your finger and create the outward lips if the latch feels good and this is the only challenge you are feeling. Most of the time, it was the top lip that my kids would not flange out. Most importantly, the latch should be comfortable for you. While the initial tug can be a bit surprising, it shouldn't be painful. If you feel discomfort, it's a sign that adjustments might be necessary.

While burping is something your breastfed baby may need to do a lot or a little depending on their latch, I wanted to share one of the ways I have been able to get my last baby to burp. Think of your baby as a straight line, so after you feed, bring your baby's head to your chest upright and pat on the back. I then would lean her back to just past being flat so that her head is a little below the level of her stomach. Then slowly bring her back to the upright position and continue to pat on the back or place her on my shoulder and pat her back. For some reason, taking her to the flat position and then back upright helped move her air bubble and allowed her to burp. My firstborn rarely burped at all that I could tell, but I still stopped part way through nursing and allowed him the opportunity to burp. My second child was a good "burper" so we did not have to get too creative to burp, but this last one, just did not want to burp for a while unless I leaned her back.

Mother's Comfort

It's a common misconception that breastfeeding is inherently painful. Yes, there's an adjustment period, and some initial tenderness is normal, but persistent pain is a red flag that the latch needs attention. Your letdown and initial weeks of breastfeeding may include some soreness and intense feelings, however, ongoing pain is a sign of something else, so pay attention to your body and act accordingly. If you're experiencing pain beyond the typical initial tenderness, it's time to unlatch and try again. Remember, each attempt is a learning experience, not just for you but for your baby as well. By the time they are two to three months old, they will be able to latch with little issues and great success.

Adjusting the Latch

If you're feeling discomfort or if the latch just doesn't seem right, don't hesitate to start over. It's entirely okay to gently insert your finger into the corner of your baby's mouth to break the suction, then try latching again. This can be a trial and error process, and that's perfectly fine. Sometimes, just shifting your baby's position slightly or ensuring that their mouth is wide open before you bring them to your breast can make all the difference.

Don't rush this process; take your time to find the position and approach that feel best for both of you. As you are working to latch, make sure your baby is facing you. Their entire body should be facing your breast.

2.2 Troubleshooting Common Latching Issues

Navigating the hurdles of latching isn't always easy, and is different for every mom. For instance, if you have flat or inverted nipples, you might find that achieving that perfect latch feels a bit more elusive. It's a common issue, and thankfully, there are reliable strategies to help. Nipple shields, for instance, can be a great aid. These thin, flexible silicone covers provide a protruding nipple shape that can help your baby latch on more easily. However, it's essential to use them under the guidance of a lactation consultant because they can affect milk transfer and supply if not used correctly. Another helpful technique involves nipple stimulation before feeding. Gently rolling your nipple between your fingers or using a breast pump for a short time can draw out the nipple, making it easier for your baby to latch. While I did not have inverted nipples, I still used the breast pump to help draw out the nipple and make sure the milk was ready for when the baby did latch properly.

Engorgement can also make latching a challenge. This occurs when your breasts are overly full with milk, making them firm and swollen which can flatten the nipple and areola, making it difficult for your baby to latch deeply. Imagine trying to get suction onto a basketball, it is nearly impossible. To alleviate engorgement and facilitate easier latching, try expressing a small amount of milk before feeding. This can soften the breast enough to help your baby get a better grip. Hand expression or a breast pump can be used for this purpose, and this can also provide some relief from the discomfort of engorgement. Remember, consistent feeding and expressing are key to managing engorgement, as they help regulate your milk production to better match your baby's needs. We will talk more about specific strategies to combat engorgement in a later chapter.

Addressing your baby's oral challenges is another crucial aspect of troubleshooting latching difficulties. Conditions like tongue-tie or lip-tie, where the tissues connecting the tongue to the floor of the mouth or the lip to the gum are too tight, can restrict the movements necessary for effective latching. These issues can not only make breastfeeding painful but can also inhibit your baby's ability to effectively remove milk, potentially affecting their weight gain and your milk supply. If you suspect your baby might have tongue-tie or lip-tie, it's important to consult with a healthcare provider who can offer a proper assessment and discuss potential treatment options, which might include a simple procedure to release the tie. This is such an easy issue to alleviate for your baby, so take the time to check into it if you have ongoing latching issues.

Lastly, the process of frequent relatching in the early days, while often frustrating, is incredibly common. It's a learning curve for both you and your baby. Each attempt at latching is an opportunity for both of you to get better at the breastfeeding process. If your baby slips off the breast or seems to struggle with maintaining a good latch, take a moment, calm yourself and your baby, and try again. This persistence pays off, as each successful latch strengthens your baby's sucking reflex and your own understanding of their needs and behaviors. Patience here is not just a virtue but a necessity.

Navigating these common latching issues successfully often involves a combination of patience, practice, and sometimes professional advice. Each challenge has a solution, often it just takes some time and trial and error to find it. As you become more adept at identifying and responding to these challenges, you'll find that each feeding becomes smoother, sometimes quicker and more fulfilling for both of you.

2.3 Breastfeeding Positions for Every Situation

Finding the right position for breastfeeding isn't just about comfort; it's about making sure your baby can latch effectively and you can maintain this activity without strain over the months. Understanding these can give you more tools in your breastfeeding toolkit, making the experience more adaptable to your daily life and physical condition.

Cradle and Cross-Cradle Hold

The cradle hold is one of the first positions that comes to mind when you think of breastfeeding. In this classic position, you cradle your baby in your arm, with their head resting comfortably in the bend of your elbow. It's a natural, intuitive posture that many mothers and babies find comforting and easy to maintain. For the cradle hold, you usually hold your baby with the arm on the same side as the nursing breast. This position is especially handy in relaxed settings where you have a good back support and can sit undisturbed for a while. On the other hand, the cross-cradle hold is slightly different and can be particularly useful for newborns and infants who need a little more head and neck support. Here, you hold your baby along the opposite arm from the breast you are nursing from. This means if you are nursing from the right breast, you use your left arm to hold your baby. This position gives you more control over how your baby is latching on because you can use your free hand to support your breast and guide your baby's mouth to the nipple. Both these positions allow for eye contact and bonding during feeding, making them not just physically but emotionally satisfying.

In the first days of my breastfeeding journeys with all three of my children, the cross cradle hold was our go-to. I held the baby's head in the palm of the opposite arm from the breast I was feeding on and was able to kind of "pinch" my nipple to allow for a good, deep latch. The cross cradle hold is what we used for about the first 4–6 weeks as the infants got stronger and were able to latch without as much support or guidance.

Football Hold

Now, if you're recovering from a cesarean delivery, have large breasts, or are nursing twins, the football hold might become your go-to. This hold involves tucking your baby under your arm (on the same side that you're nursing from) like a football or handbag. Your baby's back will rest on your forearm, and you can support their head and neck with your hand. This position keeps the baby's weight off your abdomen, which can be a significant relief if you have stitches from a cesarean section. It also provides ample room to nurse twins simultaneously, one on each side, which can be a real time-saver. The football hold offers excellent control over the baby's position and latch. Plus, it can be easier to see and correct any latching issues when you're looking down at your baby from this angle.

This is a great hold for when the baby is small, however, as they grow, it is difficult for me to keep them in the proper position. Do try this hold though, as it keeps the weight off the abdomen and also allows for the free hand to use as a guide or support for the baby or breast.

Side-Lying Position

The side-lying position is a lifesaver during night feedings or if you need rest during the day but it's time to feed your baby. To nurse in this position, lie on your side with your baby facing you, your bodies mirroring each other. You can use your lower arm to cradle your head or lay it flat, whatever feels best. This position is comfortable, relaxing, and means you can both lie down during those night feeds when getting up feels like too much of a challenge. It's also beneficial if you're recovering from delivery and need to minimize movement. Just make sure to keep your baby's face clear from the bedding and your body, ensuring they have plenty of air.

During recovery from a C-section, this position was used extensively in our home during the day as well as at night. All of my children have been co-sleepers so being able to nurse lying down has allowed me to continue to get quality rest.

Using Pillows for Support

Regardless of which breastfeeding position you choose, pillows can be your best friend. They help create comfortable setups and alleviate physical strain. In positions like the cradle or cross-cradle, a nursing pillow wrapped around your waist supports your baby's weight, which can help prevent arm and back fatigue. During the football hold, a pillow placed at your side can help raise your baby to the level of your breast, reducing the need for you to lean over. For the side-lying position, a pillow behind your back can offer stability, allowing you to lean back slightly without rolling away from your baby. Pillows can be adjusted and stacked until you find just the right configuration that keeps you and your baby snug and supported. I would recommend having several pillows of different material to ensure you get what you are looking for. I would also recommend a few toddler pillows. I used these extensively to support my elbows in a chair and they are not as bulky as full size pillows.

Each of these positions has its own advantages and can be mixed and matched throughout your day to suit different feeding needs or simply to give you a change of scenery. Remember, what works best can vary from one feed to another, depending on both your and your baby's mood and comfort. The key is to remain flexible and open to trying different positions until you find what works best for each situation.

2.4 When to Seek Help: Lactation Consultants and Support Groups

Sometimes, despite your best efforts and all the strategies you've tried, breastfeeding challenges can persist, and it's perfectly okay to feel over-whelmed or unsure. Recognizing when to seek help can make a significant difference in your breastfeeding experience, ensuring both you and your baby are healthier and happier. It's important to remember that needing help is not a sign of failure; it's a proactive step towards ensuring the best care for you and your baby. If you're consistently experiencing pain during feeds, if your baby isn't gaining weight appropriately, or if you have concerns about your milk supply, these are all valid reasons to reach out for professional support. Pain, in particular, can be a sign that something isn't quite right with the way your baby is latching on, and ignoring it can lead to further complications such as infections or a dwindling milk supply. Similarly, a baby who isn't gaining weight well might not be getting enough milk, which could be due to various manageable factors. Lastly, doubts about milk supply are incredibly common and can often be resolved with expert advice and support.

Lactation consultants specialize in breastfeeding support and can offer a wealth of knowledge and practical solutions that are tailored to your specific situation. When you schedule a consultation, expect a comprehensive session that starts with a conversation about your breastfeeding history and any challenges you're facing. The consultant will likely observe a feed to assess your baby's latch, your posture, and how you both interact during the process. This hands-on evaluation is invaluable because it can uncover issues that are not always apparent even to the most attentive mothers. Lactation consultants can provide techniques to improve the latch, suggest different breastfeeding positions to enhance comfort, and offer strategies to increase milk production if needed. Perhaps more importantly, they provide reassurance and emotional support, which can be just as crucial as practical advice.

Finding support doesn't end with professional help; connecting with other breastfeeding mothers through support groups can also be incredibly beneficial. These groups offer a platform to share experiences, tips, and encouragement. To find these groups, you can start by asking your healthcare provider for recommendations or searching for local breastfeeding networks online. Libraries, pediatric offices, and community centers often have information about local support groups. Social media offers other avenues to connect with mothers like you and ask questions about their experiences. You are not alone and are doing an outstanding job.

Sometimes, breastfeeding issues can escalate into medical concerns, such as mastitis or thrush, which are infections that require medical treatment. Mastitis is an inflammation of breast tissue that can cause pain, swelling, warmth, and redness in the breast, often accompanied by fever and chills.

Thrush is a fungal infection in your baby's mouth that can spread to your breasts and cause itching and pain. Both conditions are reasons to consult healthcare providers promptly. They can provide medical treatment and guidance to manage these conditions effectively, ensuring they don't have a lasting impact on your breastfeeding journey. Your healthcare provider can also work in tandem with your lactation consultant to provide a comprehensive plan to support your breastfeeding goals. Whether it's through professional consultants, support groups, or healthcare providers, help is available, and it can be a helpful tool ensuring success in breastfeeding.

2.5 Partner Support in the Early Days of Breastfeeding

When you're navigating the new waters of breastfeeding, having your partner's support can be like finding an anchor in choppy seas. It's not just about having someone to share the load—it's about feeling understood, valued, and cared for. Emotional support from your partner can significantly enhance your breastfeeding experience, making it less stressful and more of a shared journey. Encouragement can come in many forms: a reassuring smile, a gentle conversation, or simply the presence of someone who understands the challenges and triumphs of breastfeeding. These gestures may seem small, but they're profoundly impactful, reinforcing your confidence and emotional well-being during this sensitive period.

Practical assistance is equally crucial. Imagine it's three in the morning; you're exhausted, and your baby is awake and hungry. Now picture your partner, groggily but willingly, getting up to bring your baby to you. It's a simple act, but it means you can stay nestled under the covers a bit longer, conserving your energy for feeding. Or consider the daily routines—your partner taking on more household tasks, ensuring you're eating well and staying hydrated, or simply recognizing what you do to ensure the health of your baby. These actions alleviate your load, allowing you to focus more on your recovery and on establishing a successful breastfeeding routine.

Encouraging partners to educate themselves about breastfeeding can also make a significant difference. When partners understand why and how certain breastfeeding practices are important, they're better equipped to support you effectively. This knowledge empowers them not just to support you passively but to take an active role in ensuring the breastfeeding experience is successful.

Advocacy is another critical area where partners can play a significant role. There will be times, especially in social settings or during interactions with healthcare professionals, when you might feel too overwhelmed to speak up about your breastfeeding needs or rights. A partner who can advocate on your behalf in these situations is invaluable. Whether it's setting boundaries with family and friends regarding visit times to ensure they don't interrupt the breastfeeding schedule, or speaking up during medical appointments to make sure your breastfeeding concerns are addressed, having an advocate by your side can provide a tremendous sense of security and empowerment.

In essence, the role of a partner in the breastfeeding process extends far beyond mere help; it involves emotional connection, practical support, shared knowledge, and advocacy. As you both adapt to this new life with your little one, remember that every offer of help, every learned fact about breastfeeding, and every act of advocacy is a building block in the foundation of your family's health and happiness.

CHAPTER THREE

OVERCOMING INITIAL HURDLES

Breastfeeding, like any new skill, comes with its learning curve and set of challenges. It's perfectly normal to encounter a few bumps along the way. Think of these not as setbacks, but as opportunities to deepen your understanding and enhance your breastfeeding experience. One of the first obstacles you might face is engorgement, which can be uncomfortable and daunting. However, with the right strategies and knowledge, you can manage and even prevent it, ensuring both you and your baby continue to enjoy the benefits of breastfeeding. Let's dive into some effective ways to handle engorgement, keeping you comfortable and your baby happily fed.

3.1 Managing Engorgement: Relief and Prevention

Engorgement is that overwhelming fullness you feel in your breasts as they swell with milk, often accompanied by hardness and sometimes discomfort or pain. It typically occurs when the milk begins to "come in" properly a few days postpartum and can happen at other times when there's a mismatch between how much milk you're producing and how much your baby is consuming. While it's a sign that your body is enthusiastic about providing for your baby, the accompanying discomfort isn't exactly pleasant.

Cold Compresses and Warm Showers

To alleviate the discomfort of engorgement, alternating between cold and warm treatments can be highly effective. Cold compresses, applied after feeding, can help reduce swelling and numb the pain. You can use a chilled gel pack or even a bag of frozen peas wrapped in a thin cloth. Don't apply ice directly to your skin, as it can cause damage. On the other hand, warm showers before breastfeeding can be soothing and help the milk flow more freely. The warmth encourages milk ducts to expand, easing the flow and reducing the pressure. This gentle combination of heat and cold not only manages the symptoms but can also make breastfeeding sessions more productive and less painful.

Feeding Frequency and Duration

Regular feeding or pumping is your best defense against engorgement. Try to feed your baby on demand—whenever they show signs of hunger or at least every two to three hours. This helps to regulate your milk production based on your baby's needs and prevents milk from accumulating to uncomfortable levels. If your baby has a shorter feeding or suddenly starts sleeping longer stretches, you might need to express some milk to relieve fullness. Remember, your body is continually adjusting its milk production based on demand, so consistent feeding helps stabilize supply and reduce episodes of engorgement.

Manual Expression Techniques

Sometimes, your breasts may still become engorged despite regular feeding, especially in the early weeks as your body adjusts. Learning to express milk manually can be a game-changer. This technique involves using your hand to gently massage and compress the breast to release milk. It can relieve pressure, prevent clogged ducts, and make it easier for your baby to latch on to a softer breast. Start by massaging from the outer areas of your breast towards the nipple to encourage milk flow, then use your thumb and fingers to compress the breast gently. This skill is particularly handy during times when you're away from your baby or if you're experiencing issues with your breast pump. Another option is to hop in the warm shower to hand express. I have done this deliberately to get some relief and also kind of accidentally as I was in the shower and started releasing milk. Just know that warmth can be your friend.

Wearing Supportive, Non-restrictive Bras

The right kind of breast support can make a significant difference in how you manage engorgement. Avoid tight, restrictive bras, which can exacerbate discomfort and even lead to complications like clogged ducts. Instead, opt for supportive, well-fitting bras made of breathable material. Maternity and nursing bras are designed with these needs in mind, providing support without constricting milk flow. They often come with adjustable features that accommodate changes in your breast size and make breastfeeding more accessible, thanks to flaps or panels that can be easily opened.

With these strategies, you can prevent and address engorgement, maintaining a comfortable, healthy flow of milk. As you continue to adapt and learn, you'll find that these early hurdles soon turn into strides of confidence, making your breastfeeding experience increasingly smoother and more successful

3.2 Sore Nipple Solutions: From Prevention to Care

One of the common discomforts you might encounter while breastfeeding is sore nipples. This can be quite disheartening, especially when you're doing your best to nourish your baby. But rest assured, this issue is not only manageable but largely preventable with the right techniques and care products. Let's explore how correct latching, the use of soothing creams, and practical adjustments to your breastfeeding routine can help alleviate and prevent nipple soreness, enhancing your breastfeeding experience.

Proper latching is foundational in preventing nipple soreness. I know we have already talked about this, but as a reminder, a good latch means that your baby's mouth covers a large part of the areola below the nipple, rather than just the nipple itself as well as the lips being flanged out. This technique minimizes the tugging and compression on the nipple itself and distributes the suction more evenly across the areola. To ensure your baby is latching on correctly, aim to position your baby so that their nose is opposite your nipple, encouraging them to open wide before latching on. You can gently brush your baby's lips with your nipple to encourage them to open their mouth wide. Once they do, bring your baby quickly to your breast, chin first, allowing them to take in a good portion of the breast tissue. If the latch feels painful or too shallow, don't hesitate to gently insert your finger into the corner of your baby's mouth to break the suction, and try again. This might take a few tries, but patience here pays off greatly in terms of comfort and effective feeding.

When dealing with nipple soreness, the application of nipple creams and ointments can be extremely beneficial. Look for products that are safe for ingestion by babies, meaning you won't need to wash them off before feeding. These ointments often contain lanolin, which is excellent for soothing cracked or sore nipples due to its moisturizing properties. There are also many plant-based alternatives if you prefer a vegan option or are sensitive to lanolin. Apply a small amount after each feed to help soothe and protect your nipples. Additionally, some mothers find that applying a few drops of expressed breast milk and letting it air dry on the nipples offers a natural healing remedy, thanks to the milk's natural antibacterial properties.

Air drying and exposure can also play significant roles in preventing and healing sore nipples. After feeding, try to leave your breasts exposed to air for a little while, allowing your nipples to dry naturally before covering them again. This practice helps prevent moisture from remaining in contact with your nipples, which can exacerbate soreness and lead to infections like thrush. If you're at home and privacy allows, letting your breasts air out can be a simple yet effective technique to promote healing. I could never walk around barring all the world, but if you can, that works.

Lastly, alternating breasts and changing breastfeeding positions can help significantly in managing and preventing nipple soreness. If one nipple is particularly sore, start feeding on the less sore side to allow your baby to latch more gently when they are hungriest and sucking most vigorously. This can give the more sore nipple a bit of a break. Additionally, changing positions can help distribute the pressure and suction of breastfeeding more evenly across different areas of the breast and nipple, which can prevent any one spot from becoming overly sore. For instance, if you usually use the cradle hold, try switching to the football hold, or vice versa. Each position applies pressure in slightly different ways, so this simple change can provide much-needed relief.

I can remember sitting while feeding in the first several weeks and stomping my foot on the ground in pain while telling myself, "Don't squeeze his head, don't squeeze his head." The pain you may feel for a short term is real, even if you have a good latch. Know that it gets much better and will subside. With my most recent child, I did not even need the jars of nipple cream as my body regulated and my pain level, even at the beginning, was much less.

3.3 The Lowdown on Milk Supply: Reality vs. Myth

Understanding how your body produces milk can sometimes feel like trying to solve a complex puzzle, especially when faced with the myriad of myths surrounding milk supply. It's common to hear new moms express concerns about not having enough milk, but more often than not, these worries stem from misunderstandings about how milk production works. Let's clear that up.

Breast milk production is primarily a "supply and demand" process. This means the more your baby nurses, the more milk your body is stimulated to produce. It's a beautifully designed system that adjusts to the unique needs of your baby. However, many new moms worry when they don't feel their breasts are full, or they don't see milk leaking as a sign of abundant supply. It's important to understand that breast fullness or the lack of it isn't a reliable indicator of your milk supply. As your body becomes more attuned to your baby's needs, it regulates the production more efficiently, and your breasts might not feel as full. This doesn't mean you're producing less milk; it simply means your body is adapting to your baby's feeding pattern.

Observing your baby's behavior and growth can provide reassuring clues about your milk supply. Signs of adequate milk intake include regular wet diapers—about six or more in 24 hours with clear or very pale urine. Also, after the initial weight loss that most newborns experience, consistent weight gain is a reliable indicator. Your baby should seem content and satisfied after most feedings and will be active and alert when awake. These signs are much more indicative of sufficient milk supply than the feeling of fullness in the breasts. This is difficult to adopt as a mindset, I know. I struggled with it myself.

Boosting your milk supply naturally involves several effective strategies. Staying hydrated is crucial because your body needs enough fluids to produce milk. Make sure to drink plenty of water throughout the day; keeping a water bottle handy during feeding times is a good practice. A nursing mom should drink approximately 125-130 ounces of water daily. This seems like a high number, I know, but your body is making milk so you need something to start with to feed the baby as well as hydration for your body. Essentially, you are staying hydrated for two people. Nursing on demand rather than on a strict schedule allows your body to respond naturally to your baby's hunger cues, which can vary day by day and week by week. This helps in maintaining a supply that is perfectly tailored to your baby's needs. Additionally, incorporating lactogenic foods into your diet can also support milk production. Foods like oats, almonds, and fenugreek are known for their milk-boosting properties. While the impact of these foods can vary from person to person, they are healthy additions to your diet and worth trying.

Feeling overwhelmed with milk supply concerns is natural, but rest assured, many mothers face similar challenges. It's important to keep in mind that if your baby is content, gaining weight, and having wet diapers, your milk supply is likely sufficient. Here are some effective strategies to boost your milk production:

- **Oats**: Incorporate oats into your diet through oatmeal, oat cereals, or oatmeal creme pies. These foods are excellent for boosting milk supply.

- **Fenugreek**: This herbal supplement is rich in phytoestrogens and has been traditionally used to enhance milk production.

- **Brewer's Yeast**: Often found in lactation cookies and products, brewer's yeast provides essential nutrients like iron and B vitamins to support milk production.

- **Spinach & Leafy Greens**: These nutrient-rich greens benefit both you and your baby, contributing to increased milk supply.

- **Nuts**: Packed with healthy fats and vitamins, nuts are a nutritious option to support lactation.

Remember, a balanced diet full of nutrients is key to supporting milk production, and while numerous supplements claim to boost supply instantly, results can vary. Always consider individual differences.

Additionally, some mothers have found success with oxytocin nasal spray. While it can be effective, I urge you to consult your physician due to potential side effects. A study published in the Journal of Maternal-Fetal &

Neonatal Medicine highlights the benefits and risks, emphasizing the need for professional guidance.

Finally, consider implementing a power pumping schedule to stimulate milk production. The body's milk production operates on a supply and demand basis; the more milk you express, the more your body will produce. Gradually increase the frequency and duration of your pumping and nursing sessions. Here's a helpful schedule to follow:

- **Day 1-3**: Pump for 20 minutes every 3 hours

- **Day 4-7**: Pump for 25 minutes every 2.5 hours

- **After Day 7**: Adjust as needed based on your milk supply

A tip to ease the process: try to relax and enjoy the bonding time with your baby during nursing, as stress can hinder milk production. This schedule supported me immensely, providing thousands of ounces of milk for my children.

Knowing when to seek professional advice about your milk supply is essential. If you're concerned because your baby isn't gaining weight well or isn't producing enough wet diapers, it's important to consult with a healthcare provider or a lactation consultant. Sometimes, low milk supply can be linked to fixable issues like a poor latch or insufficient feeding frequency. Other times, it might be related to maternal health issues such as hormonal imbalances or previous breast surgeries that affect milk production. A professional can offer guidance tailored to your specific situation, providing strategies to enhance milk production or supplementary feeding advice if necessary.

Remember, each breastfeeding experience is unique, and what works for one mother might not work for another. Trust in your body, observe your baby's cues, and don't hesitate to reach out for support when needed. With patience and the right information, you'll find that you and your baby can thrive on this nurturing path.

3.4 The Impact of Postpartum Recovery on Breastfeeding

The days and weeks following the arrival of your baby are a mix of joy, challenges, and significant physical and emotional adjustments. Navigating your physical recovery while also learning to breastfeed can sometimes feel like you're handling too much at once. It's important to remember that your body has undergone a tremendous journey, and giving birth is a major event that requires ample recovery time. This recovery process can directly impact your ability to breastfeed, both physically and emotionally.

Physical recovery after giving birth varies widely from one mother to another. You might be dealing with soreness, fatigue, or more significant issues like recovery from a cesarean section. Each of these conditions can make the physical act of breastfeeding more challenging. Fatigue, for example, can make it difficult to maintain the frequent feeding schedule needed to establish a good milk supply. To manage this, consider creating a comfortable nursing station where everything you need is within easy reach. This might include a comfortable chair with support pillows, supplies for hydration and snacks, and perhaps a place to prop up your feet. Also, don't hesitate to breastfeed lying down if that's more comfortable for you, especially in the early days. This position can help you rest while your baby feeds and is particularly beneficial if you're recovering from surgery or experiencing significant postpartum pain.

The emotional health of a new mother is profoundly tied to her ability to produce milk. Stress, anxiety, and postpartum mood disorders like depression can interfere with the hormones that help produce and release breast milk. It's crucial to monitor your emotional well-being and seek support when you feel overwhelmed. Open conversations with your partner, a trusted friend, or a healthcare provider can provide emotional relief and practical support. Additionally, joining a support group for new mothers can connect you with others who understand what you're going through. These groups can be wonderful resources for companionship and sharing strategies to cope with the emotional ups and downs of new motherhood.

Rest and proper nutrition play critical roles in your postpartum recovery and your ability to breastfeed successfully. It's common to hear "sleep when the baby sleeps," and while this isn't always possible, it's important to prioritize rest whenever you can. Lack of sleep can affect your milk production and make it harder to cope with the demands of a newborn. Nutrition is equally important; eating a well-balanced diet rich in proteins, vitamins, and minerals supports your recovery and your energy levels. Foods rich in iron and calcium are particularly important postpartum. If you're struggling to find time to eat properly, consider preparing meals in advance or asking friends and family for help with meal preparation. Before going to the hospital to have my third child, I made a super rich trail mix out of cranberries, pistachios, pecans that I toasted and salted and a few other nuts. This was a lifesaver and calorie - rich food that was good for me and the baby. Additionally, I highly recommend additional fiber intake. The digestive system can be greatly impacted by childbirth, and getting it going again is a major relief.

If you encounter complications like infections or severe pain, it's essential to seek medical help promptly. Conditions such as mastitis or a uterine infection can significantly impact your ability to care for yourself and your baby, including your capacity to breastfeed. Early intervention is key to preventing more serious health issues and can help you return to a comfortable breastfeeding routine sooner. Always communicate openly with your healthcare provider about any symptoms you're experiencing, no matter how minor they may seem. Your health and comfort are crucial not only for your well-being but for your ability to provide care to your new baby.

Remember, taking care of yourself is just as important as taking care of your baby. By addressing your needs, you're setting both of you up for a healthier, happier start together.

3.5 Coping with the Emotional Rollercoaster

Breastfeeding, while full of beautiful moments, can also tug at every emotional string you possess. One minute you might feel a surge of love as you gaze into your baby's eyes, and the next, you might feel overwhelmed by frustration or doubt if things don't go as planned. It's important to know that experiencing this wide range of emotions is completely normal and you're definitely not alone in feeling this way. Many new mothers find themselves riding this emotional rollercoaster, especially in the early stages of breastfeeding when everything is still new and you're likely adjusting to a significant lack of sleep.

One effective way to manage these feelings is through mindfulness techniques. Simple practices like deep breathing or meditation can be done almost anywhere and require only a few minutes. When you feel overwhelmed, try focusing on your breath, guiding each inhale and exhale to be slower and deeper than the last. While the idea of meditation is great, if you have multiple kids, it can be a real challenge. I found myself frantic to do one thing and then the next just to survive. At the end of the day, you just have to resolve yourself that you will make it through the difficult times and get your sanity back later. I am happy to report that those feelings do get better, so hang in there. Another technique is progressive muscle relaxation, which involves tensing and then relaxing different muscle groups in your body. This not only helps release physical tension but can also bring a sense of calm to your mind.

Seeking social support is another cornerstone of managing stress and emotional upheaval. Talking through your feelings with a partner, friend, or family member can provide relief and often, practical solutions. Sometimes, just voicing your worries can lighten your emotional load. Moreover, connecting with other breastfeeding mothers, either in person or online, can offer the reassurance that what you're experiencing is normal and that you're doing just fine. These connections can be incredibly validating and provide a reservoir of shared wisdom and encouragement. Find your inner circle. I have a remarkable inner circle of friends that hear the worst of my thoughts and support me through those thoughts. Many women have been precisely where you are and have felt what you are feeling, you just need to tap into that knowledge and strength.

Self-care is crucial during this period, though it's often easier said than done. Try to carve out small pockets of time for yourself each day. It could be a warm bath, a short walk, reading a book, or any activity that rejuvenates you. Remember, taking care of yourself is not an act of selfishness; rather, it's an essential part of being a good mother. When you are mentally and physically well, you are better equipped to care for your baby and meet the demands of motherhood. As I welcomed our third child to the world, my two boys had a great deal of learning to do to understand that she was small and fragile and that mom had to pay her extra attention. Those times are tough. For me, my self care was getting to spend time with my other children and enjoy seeing them interact with our new little girl.

Being aware of the signs of postpartum depression and anxiety is vital. If you find yourself feeling persistently sad or hopeless, or if you're experiencing severe anxiety that interferes with your daily life, these could be signs of a deeper issue. Other symptoms might include changes in your appetite, feelings of worthlessness, or lack of interest in the baby. Postpartum depression is a serious condition, but it is treatable. Recognizing these signs early and seeking professional help can make a significant difference in your recovery. Healthcare providers can offer resources, support, and sometimes medication or therapy, which can help you navigate these challenges more effectively.

Navigating the emotional landscape of breastfeeding is no small feat, but with the right tools and support, you can manage these feelings effectively. Embrace the good moments, learn from the challenges, and remember that with each day, you're doing an incredible job. As we wrap up this chapter, remember that the emotional rollercoaster of breastfeeding is a natural part of the journey. The bond, built through both the highs and the lows, becomes a source of strength and joy for both of you as you continue to grow together.

CHAPTER FOUR

BREASTFEEDING AND HEALTH

Navigating the nutritional landscape during breastfeeding can sometimes feel like trying to solve a complex puzzle with your health and your baby's well-being at stake. You're not just eating for energy anymore; your body is now a nutrition powerhouse, churning out the perfect baby food: breast milk. But let's be real, understanding and managing your dietary needs while breastfeeding isn't always simple.

4.1 Nutritional Needs for Breastfeeding Moms

Caloric Intake and Quality

When you're breastfeeding, your body requires more calories. Not just a few more—but up to an additional 500 calories per day could be needed to fuel milk production. It's like running a small marathon each day without having to leave your comfy sofa or rocking chair! But it's not just about eating more; it's about eating smart. The quality of the calories you consume matters immensely. Nutrient-dense foods—those packed with vitamins, minerals, and other nutrients important for both you and your baby—are crucial. Think whole grains, lean proteins, healthy fats, and plenty of fruits and vegetables. These foods do double duty: they provide the energy you need to keep up with the demands of new motherhood and support the nutritional content of your breast milk.

Essential Vitamins and Minerals

While your body is quite adept at managing its resources to produce nutritious milk for your baby, certain vitamins and minerals are essential for lactation and need to be included in your diet. Calcium, iron, and vitamin D are stars here. Calcium supports your baby's skeletal development, and if you're not taking in enough, your body will leach it from your own bones, which isn't ideal and can lead to arthritis and other bone density issues later in life. . Dairy products, green leafy vegetables, and fortified foods are great sources. Iron helps keep your energy levels up and prevents anemia, a common postpartum concern. Include lean meats, beans, and fortified cereals in your meals. Vitamin D is crucial for both you and your baby, aiding in bone strength and immune function. Sun exposure can help boost vitamin D levels, but dietary sources like fatty fish or fortified milk and a suitable supplement can ensure you're getting enough.

Supplementation

Sometimes, even the best diets need a little help. This is where supplements come into play. If you're concerned about filling any nutritional gaps, a well-balanced multivitamin or supplements specifically designed for breastfeeding women can be beneficial. Omega-3 fatty acids, particularly DHA, are important for your baby's brain development and might not always be consumed in sufficient quantities through diet alone, especially if you don't eat fish regularly. Consulting with a healthcare provider can give you personalized advice on what supplements might be beneficial based on your dietary intake and nutritional needs. Throughout pregnancy and breastfeeding, I have always taken a prenatal with DHA. Another concept to discuss here is fiber. While it may seem like a simple concept, getting enough fiber and keeping your system moving is a top priority. I use a fiber gummy to ensure I reach the fiber recommendations; however, most people do not have adequate fiber in their diets.

Nutrition transfer to Breastmilk

The time it takes for what you eat or drink to transfer into breastmilk varies based on the substance and your metabolism, with some substances entering breastmilk in as little as one hour. According to a study published in the Journal of Human Lactation, caffeine, for example, reaches breastmilk within one to two hours post-consumption. This timing is particularly critical if your baby has sensitivities.

For instance, I attended a social event where I ate just one jalapeño popper. Only an hour later, during my baby girl's feeding, she became unusually fussy and cried. She remained uncomfortable through the night and into the next morning. I'm convinced it was a reaction to the jalapeño, as I have avoided spicy foods since her birth. The popper seemed mild, so I thought it would be fine, but evidently, it was not.

Regarding dairy, I found that all my children, along with many other parents I've spoken with, experienced sensitivities to dairy in their early months. With my second and third child, I limited dairy intake in the weeks leading up to and following their births. Dairy products can take a week or more to fully clear from your system and breastmilk. Therefore, I suggest starting with a bland diet, gradually introducing small amounts of foods known for causing potential sensitivities, so you can determine if your baby has a reaction.

Balanced Diet Examples

Let's put all this into a practical context with some examples of balanced meals and snacks that can support your lactation journey. For breakfast, think about a bowl of oatmeal topped with almonds and berries, paired with a glass of fortified orange juice. This meal packs a punch with fiber, vitamin C, antioxidants, and calcium. For lunch, a quinoa salad with chickpeas, mixed greens, and slices of grilled chicken can cover your bases for protein, iron, and folic acid. Snacks are important too; yogurt with a sprinkle of flaxseed or a smoothie with spinach, banana, and a scoop of protein powder can be both refreshing and nourishing. These meal ideas satisfy your hunger and supply a rich array of nutrients to support your health and your baby's development.

If you are like me, the idea of meal planning like this is a goal... but not always a reality. I tend to eat on the move most of the time with my best meal being our evening meal as a family. During the day, I am sure to notice what I am eating and try to diversify my nutrition. Make good choices. While those french fries and fried chicken are fine to have, make sure you are including some rich colored fruits and veggies or salads. Even at fast food restaurants, there are ways to get a variety of foods. You can do this. It is best for you and best for your baby.

4.2 Foods to Favor and Avoid While Breastfeeding

Navigating your diet during breastfeeding can feel a bit like walking a tightrope. You're balancing what fuels your body and what gets passed on to your baby through your milk. Understanding which foods can enhance milk production and which ones to avoid can help you maintain this balance while ensuring your baby's well-being.

Lactogenic Foods

Let's talk about lactogenic foods, or galactagogues, which are known for their potential to boost milk supply. While the effect can vary from person to person, incorporating these foods into your diet can be beneficial. Beyond the commonly known oats and almonds, consider adding barley, which is rich in beta-glucans known to support lactation. Similarly, papaya, both green and ripe, has been traditionally used in many cultures to enhance milk production. These foods are not only nutritious but can also add variety and flavor to your meals. For instance, a stir-fry with green papaya or a barley salad can be both satisfying and beneficial for your milk supply. It's about making small, delicious tweaks to your diet that can have a positive effect on your breastfeeding experience. Here is my personal top 10 foods for breastfeeding:

- Oatmeal (a great complex carb and can be dressed up with fruit, or nuts)

- Yogurt (I also like cottage cheese for vitamins, calcium and protein)

- Spinach (rich in iron, folate and potassium as well as vitamins A, C and K)

- Flax Seeds (can be added to oatmeal, salads or trail mix blends for digestive support)

- Almonds & other Nuts (pistachios, pecans and cashews are my favorite)

- Dried Cranberries (1/2 sugar ones are high in fiber)

- Quinoa: (One of the most nutritious grains in the world. Use rice instead of rice.)

- Strawberries (My favorite, but any raw fruits are great)

- Boiled Eggs (can be added to so many dishes or eaten by themselves)

- Whole chicken (I often cooked a whole chicken then used it for various meals like chicken salad, dumplings and others)

Foods and Substances to Limit

While it's important to know what to add to your diet, it's equally crucial to understand what to limit. Caffeine, for instance, is a stimulant that you don't need to avoid completely, but moderation is key. A cup or two of coffee a day is generally considered safe, but more than that might lead to restlessness and irritability in your baby, and potentially disrupt their sleep patterns. Alcohol is another substance that should be consumed with caution. If you choose to drink, wait two to three hours per drink before breastfeeding to allow the alcohol to metabolize out of your system. This way, its impact on your baby is minimized. Certain herbs and spices, like peppermint, parsley, and sage, may reduce milk supply if consumed in large quantities. While they're fine to use in normal culinary amounts, taking them as supplements or in large doses could be counterproductive if you're trying to maintain or increase your milk production. Just a note here about spicy foods. While they are completely safe for baby and historically do not affect milk supply, all of my kids were sensitive to spicy foods while I breastfed. Just pay attention as you eat different foods to how your baby reacts and you will develop your own list of foods you need to stay away from.

Allergens and Baby's Reactions

Understanding potential allergens is crucial, as some babies might be sensitive to specific proteins in your diet, which can pass into your breast milk. Common culprits include cow's milk, soy, wheat, eggs, peanuts, tree nuts, and fish. Signs of a reaction can include excessive fussiness, a rash, eczema, or gastrointestinal symptoms such as gas, or green, mucousy stools. If you suspect your baby might be reacting to something in your diet, consider keeping a food diary to track what you eat along with any symptoms your baby exhibits. This can help you and your healthcare provider pinpoint potential allergens. If an elimination diet is recommended, it should be done under professional guidance to ensure both you and your baby are still getting all the necessary nutrients.

While it is not an allergy, babies can have reactions to hormonal changes and develop a rash. Two of my three had a terrible hormone rash all over their body, especially their faces, about 2 weeks after birth. The rash is not uncomfortable for them so try not to worry too much about it. As your hormones regulate, your milk will contain less of the hormones that cause those breakouts and they will subside.

Safe Medications while breastfeeding

You are human! You will likely have a need to take some medication sometime during your breastfeeding journey. I have included below my list of "safe" medication while breastfeeding. Safe does not mean that they do not transfer to your breastmilk, it just means that they are not proven to cause harm to a breastfed baby. As always, you need to consult with a medical professional before taking medication as I am not a doctor.

1. Pain Relievers
- Acetaminophen (Tylenol)
- Ibuprofen (Advil, Motrin)
- Naproxen (Aleve- Limited use is OK)

2. Antibiotics
- Penicillins (e.g., Amoxicillin)
- Cephalosporins (e.g., Cephalexin)
- Erythromycin

3. Allergy Medications
- Loratadine (Claritin)
- Cetirizine (Zyrtec)
- Sudafed (may reduce milk supply, so only take if absolutely necessary)

4. Cold Medications
- Guaifenesin (Mucinex)
- Dextromethorphan (Robitussin, Delsym)

5. Heartburn Medications

- Famotidine (Pepcid)

- Omeprazole (Prilosec)

6. Constipation Medications

– Ispaghol Husk

- Docusate sodium (Colace)

- Polyethylene glycol (Miralax)

8. Antifungal Medications

- Miconazole (Monistat)

- Clotrimazole (Lotrimin)

9. Asthma Medications

- Albuterol (Proventil, Ventolin)

- Inhaled corticosteroids (e.g., Fluticasone)

10. Mental Health Medications

- Sertraline (Zoloft)

- Paroxetine (Paxil)

While we are discussing medication, I would like to point out that there are a number of medications that have not been tested because of the potential risks and those medicines are not "labeled" for use while breastfeeding, but that does not necessarily mean they will be harmful. When I was in the hospital with my last child, there was medication that I needed and the "recommendation" on the label was to not breastfeed for 3 days after taking the medication. I was able to speak to the pharmacist and multiple doctors at the hospital who all indicated that the label was that way because of the lack of testing. They all said that if it were them, they would take the medication and still feed their baby, which ultimately is what was done and neither me, nor my little one were negatively affected by it. Do your research, listen to the experts and make the decisions you believe is best.

Medications that are considered safe during breastfeeding often fall under the "L1" classification according to the Lactation Risk Categories. This category signifies the "safest" drugs, having been used by a large number of breastfeeding individuals without any observed adverse effects on the infant. If you are uncertain whether a medication is safe to use while breastfeeding, look for this classification symbol on the medication label or consult with a healthcare provider to ensure safety for both you and your baby. Always prioritize informed decisions by thoroughly checking sources and consulting experts when in doubt.

Cultural Dietary Practices

Embracing cultural dietary practices can enrich your breastfeeding experience while honoring traditions that have been passed down through generations. Many cultures have specific foods that are favored during the postpartum period, often based on their properties to enhance recovery and milk production. For example, in many parts of Asia, seaweed soup is consumed because it's rich in iodine and other minerals essential for recovery and milk production. Hispanic cultures often turn to atole, a warm beverage made from masa, cinnamon, and sometimes chocolate, which is not only comforting but also calorie and nutrient-dense. Respecting and incorporating these practices can provide not only nutritional benefits but also a deep sense of connection to your heritage, which is a beautiful part of the postpartum experience.

4.3 The Role of Hydration in Milk Production

Staying well-hydrated is like oiling the gears of a machine; it keeps everything running smoothly, especially when it comes to breastfeeding. Hydration is a key player in milk production, and understanding its impact can help you maintain an ample milk supply for your baby. When you are well-hydrated, your body can produce milk more efficiently because breast milk is made up of about 90% water. On the flip side, dehydration can lead to a decrease in milk supply, making it crucial to keep up with your fluid intake throughout the day.

Water is your best friend here, and the recommendation is to take it in evenly all day instead of large quantities at once. It ensures a steady supply of the necessary fluids your body needs to produce milk and prevents the dips in supply that can happen when you're not drinking enough. How do you know if you're drinking enough? Well, your body has a fantastic way of signaling hydration levels. Dark yellow or amber-colored urine is a telltale sign you need to up your fluid intake. Ideally, your urine should be pale yellow or almost clear. Another simple indicator is how often you go to the bathroom. Less frequent bathroom trips or only going small amounts can also suggest it's time to drink more fluids.

Now, let's talk specifics about how much fluid you should be taking in. While the common advice is to drink eight glasses of water a day, when you're breastfeeding, you might need more than that. A good rule of thumb is to drink at least eight ounces of water every time you breastfeed. This doesn't mean water is your only option. Incorporating a variety of fluids can make this goal more enjoyable and achievable. Milk and juice are also hydrating, and they come with the added bonus of providing nutrients that are beneficial both for you and your baby. However, it's wise to keep an eye on your intake of caffeinated beverages like coffee and tea. While they do contribute to your fluid intake, caffeine can act as a diurean, which means it can cause your body to eliminate fluids. So, balancing these with plenty of water and other non-caffeinated beverages is key.

Here are a few practical tips to make sure you are getting enough water intake:

- Carry a water bottle- if you have water within reach, you are more likely to drink it.

- If you find it hard to remember, set a reminder on your phone, or get an app that tracks it for you.

- Have a full glass of water close to you during breastfeeding sessions and drink it while your baby feeds.

- Eat foods with a high water content like melons, oranges, cucumbers, tomatoes, lettuce, etc

These are just a few of the tips that I have used to make sure I get enough water while breastfeeding. Among them, having water bottles accessible and with me all the time has proven to be the most effective. If you do not like plain water, add a little lime or lemon juice and a tiny bit of sea salt. This mixture is nature's Gatorade and while I like to drink plain water, when you are drinking so much, mixing it up can be helpful. Try to drink at least 120 ounces of water daily to make sure you are fully hydrated.

4.4 Recognizing and Treating Mastitis at Home

Your health is of the utmost importance during this critical time. Mastitis can be one of the more daunting challenges you may face while breastfeeding. It's not just the discomfort, but the worry about what it means for your ability to continue nursing effectively. Knowing the symptoms and how to manage them can make a significant difference, not just to your health, but also to your peace of mind. Mastitis often starts as a painful area in one breast and can be accompanied by redness and swelling. You might feel a hard lump or a wedge-shaped area of engorgement. These physical symptoms are frequently coupled with flu-like symptoms such as a fever, chills, and a feeling of being run down. It's your body's way of telling you that something's off, and it's important to listen and respond promptly to these signals.

When it comes to managing mastitis at home, several strategies can be very effective in relieving symptoms and preventing the condition from worsening. One of the first steps is to apply warm compresses to the affected area. This can help soothe the discomfort and promote circulation, which in turn can help clear any blockages in your milk ducts. You can use a warm, wet washcloth or a heating pad on a low setting, but be sure to wrap it in a cloth to protect your skin. Frequent nursing or pumping from the affected breast is also crucial. It might feel counterintuitive to nurse when it's painful, but emptying the breast is one of the best ways to clear the infection and heal. Try to nurse more frequently, starting with the affected side if possible, as the stronger sucking at the beginning of a feed can help clear the blockage. Although it sounds strange, milk is not affected by mastitis, so you can continue to feed and pump like normal.

Rest is another key component of your recovery from mastitis. It can be difficult to find time to rest with a new baby, but giving your body a chance to recover is important for your overall health and milk production. When you can, sleep when your baby sleeps or ask family or friends to help with other tasks so you can focus on resting and healing. My mastitis experience was short but so painful. One major key is to catch it early, so if you begin seeing the symptoms, act sooner rather than later.

If your symptoms are persistent, getting worse, or accompanied by a fever that doesn't go down, it's important to seek medical care. Sometimes mastitis can lead to an abscess or require antibiotic treatment, and those are not issues to tackle on your own. A healthcare provider can assess your condition and prescribe antibiotics if necessary. They can also provide guidance on how to manage your symptoms and prevent complications. It's important to follow their advice closely and complete any prescribed course of treatment to ensure that the infection is fully resolved.

Preventing future episodes of mastitis is key once you've experienced it. Ensuring proper breastfeeding techniques can help prevent the milk stasis that often leads to infection. Make sure your baby is latching on well and that you're changing positions frequently to fully drain all areas of the breast. Avoid tight clothing or bras that could constrict milk flow, and try not to skip feedings or go too long between them, even if it means waking up to pump during the night. If you start to feel symptoms of engorgement or blockages, treat them promptly by applying heat, increasing feedings, and ensuring you're resting and staying hydrated. By taking these steps, you can reduce your risk of mastitis.

4.5 The Truth About Breastfeeding and Weight Loss

One of the aspects often discussed in postpartum health is how breast-feeding might influence weight loss. It's a topic that generates much interest because of the widespread belief that breastfeeding helps you shed pregnancy weight faster due to the extra calories your body burns to produce milk. While it's true that breastfeeding can increase your caloric expenditure—approximately an additional 500 calories a day—it's essential to set realistic expectations about postpartum weight loss.

Understanding how breastfeeding impacts weight loss starts with recognizing the body's increased energy demands to produce milk. This natural process is designed to ensure that you can nourish your baby adequately, which in turn, does use additional energy. However, this doesn't always equate to weight loss. Every woman's body responds differently depending on various factors, including metabolism, activity level, and overall diet. For some, the weight might seem to melt away, while for others, the scale might not budge. It's important to remember that weight loss during this time should be gradual and steady. The focus should be on recovery and health, rather than bouncing back to your pre-pregnancy weight immediately.

Talk about healthy postpartum weight loss rates—it's generally safe to lose about 1 to 1.5 pounds per week after the initial postpartum period. This rate ensures that you're losing fat rather than muscle, and it gives your skin time to adjust to the changes in your body's shape. Rapid weight loss can be a concern, especially if it affects your energy levels and overall health. If you're breastfeeding, a drastic drop in your calorie intake can also impact your milk supply, making it crucial to focus on gradual weight loss.

The emphasis should always be on nutritious eating rather than calorie counting. Restricting calories too much can not only affect your milk production but can also delay recovery from childbirth. Your body needs a good mix of protein, carbohydrates, and fats to heal and provide the nutrients necessary for breast milk. Instead of cutting calories, aim to eat a balanced diet rich in whole foods that can support both your health and your baby's growth. Incorporate various fruits, vegetables, whole grains, lean proteins, and healthy fats into your meals. These foods provide the vitamins, minerals, and antioxidants needed to support your body's recovery and the demands of breastfeeding.

As we wrap up this section on breastfeeding and health, remember that postpartum nutrition and weight management is deeply personal and varies for every mother. The focus should always be on what is best for your health and your baby's well-being. As you move forward, carry with you the understanding and practices that support a balanced diet, adequate hydration, and a realistic approach to postpartum weight changes.

In the next chapter, we'll shift our focus to adapting to your growing baby, exploring how breastfeeding evolves as your baby gets older and how to navigate the introduction of solid foods, different sleeping arrangements, and other developmental milestones. Each stage brings new challenges and joys, and being prepared can help you continue breastfeeding successfully.

Your Words Can Change a Mom's World

"Sometimes the smallest step in the right direction ends up being the biggest step of your life. Tiptoe if you must, but take the step." - Naeem Callaway

Helping even in small ways can make a big difference. It brings joy and fulfillment to both parties. Would you help a mom you've never met, even without her knowing?

Imagine a new mom—eager, yet overwhelmed. My mission is to give her confidence in her breastfeeding journey, which is where your help matters. People read books based on reviews, and your review can make a significant impact.

Please take a moment to leave a review for this book. Your words could help...

...one more mom feels supported and understood.

...one more mom finds the advice she needs to succeed.

...one more baby will thrive with the nourishment only a mom can provide.

...one more family experiences the bond that breastfeeding brings.

Simply scan the QR code below to leave your review:

If helping a mom you don't know makes you smile, you're definitely one of us. Welcome to the community. I can't wait to share more tips and strategies with you in the upcoming chapters to make your breastfeeding journey smoother and more joyful than you can imagine.

Thank you from the bottom of my heart. Now, let's dive back into your guide to breastfeeding.

With love and support, Alexandra Veal

CHAPTER FIVE

ADAPTING TO YOUR GROWING BABY

As your baby grows and begins to explore the world more actively, your breastfeeding relationship will evolve too. One of the most dynamic phases you'll encounter is when your baby goes through growth spurts and cluster feedings. These periods are marked by rapid physical and developmental changes that can significantly affect their feeding patterns. Understanding these phases and knowing how to adapt can help you maintain not only your milk supply but also your sanity.

5.1 Navigating Growth Spurts and Cluster Feedings

Understanding Growth Spurts

Growth spurts are periods when your baby seems to grow overnight, and their nutritional needs skyrocket. Typically, these spurts can occur at around two weeks, six weeks, three months, and six months of age, though they don't follow a strict timetable. During these times, you might notice that your baby is hungrier than usual, often fussier, and seems glued to your breast - feeding far more frequently than usual. This sudden increase in appetite is your baby's natural way of fueling their rapid growth and development. While it can be exhausting to keep up with, knowing that these spurts are temporary and are signs of your baby's healthy development can provide some comfort.

Managing Cluster Feedings

Cluster feedings often accompany growth spurts. This is when your baby might want to nurse almost every hour or even more frequently during certain parts of the day, usually during the evenings. It's as if they're having a series of mini-meals, which can be tiring and sometimes overwhelming. The key to managing these intense periods is to go with the flow—literally. Try to relax into these demanding phases by setting up a comfortable nursing area where you can sit back with support pillows, keep snacks and a water bottle within reach, and perhaps have a book or TV remote handy. Remember, cluster feeding is also your baby's way of boosting your milk supply to meet their growing needs, so frequent nursing during these times is absolutely normal and beneficial.

Maintaining Supply and Sanity

Keeping your milk supply up and your spirits high during these demanding periods involves more than just frequent nursing. Hydration and proper nutrition are crucial for maintaining milk production. Make sure you're drinking plenty of fluids throughout the day; a glass of water or a hydrating snack during or after each nursing session can help. Also, try to grab naps whenever possible. Sleep when your baby sleeps may sound like clichéd advice, but it's grounded in practicality—rest is essential for your well-being and by extension, your ability to produce milk and care for your baby. Just remember that it is a temporary situation.

Setting Expectations

Finally, setting realistic expectations about breastfeeding during growth spurts and cluster feedings can help you cope better. These phases are not permanent. They are simply your baby's way of navigating through their developmental milestones. Expect that some days (and nights) will be tougher and remind yourself that you're doing an incredible job. It's also helpful to keep a sense of humor about the unpredictability of it all. Laughing over the fact that your little one seems to think 'all-you-can-eat buffet' is the new routine can be surprisingly therapeutic. Talk to friends about it and keep your spirits up. Your body will adapt as needed to fit your baby's needs.

5.2 Introducing Solid Foods While Continuing to Breastfeed

When your once tiny newborn starts showing curiosity about your dinner plate, it might be time to think about introducing solid foods. This is a thrilling stage in your baby's growth that often begins around the six-month mark. Recognizing the signs that your baby is ready to expand their diet can help you start this transition confidently. Developmental readiness for solids can include being able to sit up with minimal support, showing good neck and head control, and displaying curiosity about food, such as reaching out to grab food items. Another key indicator is the loss of the tongue-thrust reflex(spitting out foods), which initially helps prevent infants from choking by pushing foreign objects (including initially unfamiliar solid foods) out of their mouth. When your baby starts keeping more in their mouth than they push out, it's a good hint they may be ready to try some solids.

Introducing solids is termed 'complementary feeding' because these foods complement the breast milk, not replace it. Breast milk should remain your baby's primary source of nutrition for the first year. When you start, think of solids as an addition to their diet, not a substitution. It's about enhancing their nutritional intake and exposing them to new tastes and textures, which helps in their development. Begin with small amounts of a single-ingredient purées. This might be something as simple as mashed banana or avocado, or single-grain cereals mixed with a bit of breast milk to make them more palatable and familiar. Gradually, as your baby becomes more accustomed to these new foods, you can increase the variety and quantity. You can also mix breastmilk with puréed fruits and veggies, so there is a little familiarity to it. Mixing breastmilk with purées also reduces thickness, which is how I got my first two children to eat solids in the beginning.

Choosing the first foods and introducing allergenic foods safely are critical steps in this journey. Starting with iron-rich foods is often recommended because, by around six months, the iron stores a baby is born with start to deplete. Pureed meats, fortified cereals, and legumes are good options. Introducing allergenic foods like peanuts, tree nuts, eggs, cow's milk products, seafood, and soy can be more daunting. Current guidelines suggest introducing these foods early and often, as this can actually help decrease the risk of developing food allergies. Start with just a tiny amount, and if there's no adverse reaction, gradually increase the quantity over future feedings. Keep a close eye on any signs of a reaction, such as hives, rash, difficulty breathing, or gastrointestinal upset. If you notice any of these, discontinue the food and consult your pediatrician. They might refer you to an allergist for further testing or provide guidance on how to safely manage food allergies.

Most of the time, it takes several times trying the same food for a baby to determine that they do or do not like it. Offer the same food multiple times before deciding that your child does not like it. I liked to offer it every other day for two weeks. Then if they still did not like it, I would wait a few weeks and offer it again. It seems odd but most of the time, on the second or third try, they decide to eat it. Just stick with it. Keep trying different foods, and you will have a good eater as they grow.

5.3 Night Weaning: Strategies and Considerations

Night weaning your baby can feel like a significant milestone in your parenting journey. It's a step that can potentially lead to more restful nights for you and your baby, but it's important to approach this transition with care and thoughtfulness to ensure it's smooth and stress-free for everyone involved. Before you begin night weaning, consider a few crucial factors like your baby's age, their nutritional needs, and how ready your family is for this change. Most experts suggest that it's best to wait until your baby is at least six months old because younger infants still need nighttime feedings for essential nutrition and development. Also, evaluate how well your baby is eating during the day; babies who consume more solids and a variety of foods are often better candidates for night weaning. Your baby still needs the same number of calories, we just want them to get more of those calories during the day, instead of at night. Additionally, think about your family's current sleeping arrangements and routines—any significant changes, like starting daycare, a family move, or sickness, might warrant postponing night weaning until routines stabilize.

Coping with resistance is part and parcel of night weaning, as it is with any change in a baby's routine. Your baby may protest the changes, especially if they're used to nursing to sleep. Prepare yourself for a few challenging nights; this is normal and doesn't mean you're doing anything wrong. What can help significantly during these times is having alternative soothing techniques ready. Rocking, cuddling, soft singing, or playing calm music can be effective. Some parents find that having the non-nursing parent help with night waking can be particularly effective, as the baby may not expect to be nursed back to sleep. This can also be a wonderful opportunity for bonding between the baby and the other parent. Remember, flexibility is key. There will be nights when sticking strictly to your plan won't be possible—sickness, teething, or just bad days can mean that a night feed is necessary for comfort. Being adaptable doesn't mean you've failed; rather, it shows you're responsive to your baby's needs.

Night weaning isn't just a process of reducing nighttime feedings; it's about gently guiding your baby towards longer stretches of sleep while ensuring they continue to receive all the love and nutrition they need. Nighttime is when our bodies repair and recover from the day, so the longer stretches of sleep are beneficial to the baby's overall health. I have to say that all three of my children nursed during the night until they were almost one. Do what works best for you. If nursing your baby at night makes you happy, do it until you want to stop. If you want to stop nursing at night, commit to a plan and do it. Remember, each small step towards longer stretches of sleep is progress, and soon, more restful nights will likely be a reality for your family.

5.4 Co-Sleeping Pros and Cons

Co-sleeping with a newborn baby is a topic that often sparks strong opinions among parents, and for good reason. On one hand, co-sleeping can foster a deep sense of closeness between parents and their baby, making nighttime feedings more convenient and helping both parent and child get more rest. On the other hand, there are significant risks associated with co-sleeping, particularly if safe practices aren't followed. Understanding both the pros and cons can help you make an informed decision that's right for your family.

One of the biggest advantages of co-sleeping is the ease with which you can respond to your baby's needs throughout the night. Whether it's feeding, comforting, or simply being there for them when they stir, having your baby close by can make those night time wake-ups a bit less disruptive. Co-sleeping can also promote bonding, as physical closeness can help your baby feel secure and loved, which may lead to better sleep patterns over time. Additionally, many parents find that they themselves sleep more soundly knowing their baby is right next to them. However, the key to reaping these benefits is to practice safe co-sleeping.

Safe co-sleeping involves several important guidelines. First and foremost, it's crucial to create a sleep environment that minimizes risks. This means using a firm mattress without any loose bedding, pillows, or stuffed animals that could pose a suffocation hazard. It's also recommended that parents never co-sleep if they're under the influence of alcohol, drugs, or any medication that might impair their ability to wake up. Additionally, the baby should be placed on their back to sleep, and it's safer to co-sleep with your baby in a bassinet or sidecar crib attached to your bed rather than in the bed itself. Despite these precautions, there are still risks, including the potential for accidental suffocation or entrapment, which is why it's vital to weigh both the pros and cons carefully.

Pros of Co-Sleeping:

- Easier Nighttime Feedings: With your baby close by, you can respond quickly to their hunger cues without fully waking up, leading to more rest overall.

- Enhanced Bonding: Physical closeness can strengthen the emotional bond between you and your baby, which may help them feel more secure.

- Improved Sleep for Parents: Knowing your baby is safe and close can give you peace of mind, potentially leading to better sleep.

- Regulation of Baby's Breathing and Temperature: Being near parents can help regulate a newborn's breathing and temperature.

- Reduced Stress for Baby: The proximity to a parent can reduce stress levels in newborns, leading to fewer crying episodes.

Cons of Co-Sleeping:

- Risk of Suffocation or SIDS: If safe sleep guidelines aren't followed, co-sleeping increases the risk of Sudden Infant Death Syndrome (SIDS) and accidental suffocation.

- Disrupted Sleep for Parents: Some parents find that they sleep more lightly or wake up more often when sharing a bed with their baby.

- Difficulty Transitioning to Crib: Babies who co-sleep may have a harder time transitioning to sleeping independently in a crib.

- Potential for Accidental Injury: There's a risk of parents rolling over onto the baby or the baby becoming trapped between the mattress and the bed frame.

- Strain on Parental Relationship: Sharing a bed with a baby can sometimes lead to less privacy and intimacy for the parents.

Ultimately, the decision to co-sleep is a personal one that should be made after carefully considering both the benefits and the potential risks. The establishment medical community recommends having a baby sleep on their back in a crib with a firm mattress and no blankets or other items in the crib. I have not been able to achieve that with any of my children yet. I do have many friends in our group that were able to get their kids in their own crib with minimal problems. If you do choose to co-sleep, following safe practices is essential to protecting your baby's health and well-being. Whatever you do, make sure you are following the recommendations for safe sleep for you and your baby.

5.5 When and How to Introduce a Bottle

Introducing a bottle to a breastfed baby comes with its own set of considerations and learning curves, but often is a great point of anxiety for moms that want their baby to have breast milk exclusively. The timing of this introduction can significantly influence your ongoing breastfeeding journey, making it crucial to approach this step thoughtfully. Ideally, you'll want to wait until breastfeeding is well-established, which typically means your baby is about 4 to 6 weeks old. That is not always possible as you may have to go back to work and want to ensure the baby is comfortable with the bottle before that time comes.

Bottle feeding, much like breastfeeding, is a skill that requires patience and practice. For many babies, the switch between a breast and a bottle isn't just about continuing to receive milk; it's about adapting to a different flow rate, nipple shape, and feeding technique. When introducing a bottle, choose a time when your baby is calm and not overly hungry, as they might be too frustrated to try something new. You might find it easier to have someone else, like your partner or a caregiver, give the first few bottle feedings, as babies can smell their mother and might refuse a bottle in favor of breastfeeding. This can also be a wonderful opportunity for bonding between your baby and other family members. To preserve your milk supply and continue the breastfeeding relationship, consider using paced bottle feeding. This technique involves holding the bottle horizontally and allowing the baby to draw milk out at their own pace, mimicking the breastfeeding experience. This method encourages the baby to suck, swallow, and breathe as they do at the breast, which can help prevent overfeeding and minimize confusion. It's important to continue regular breastfeeding sessions, especially in the morning and at night, to ensure that your milk supply remains robust.

Nipple confusion, or nipple preference, occurs when a baby develops a preference for the bottle over the breast, often because milk flows more quickly from a bottle. To minimize this risk, select a slow-flow nipple for bottle feedings to better replicate the breastfeeding experience. Also, be mindful of how often you offer a bottle. Consistently alternating between breast and bottle can help your baby adapt to both methods without developing a strong preference for one. If you notice a reluctance to breastfeed after introducing a bottle, it might be necessary to cut back on bottle use and focus on breastfeeding skills until your baby is more adaptable. In the 3-6 week timeframe, I introduced a bottle by holding the baby in the cross-cradle hold and using my extra hand to place the bottle close to my breast, so my baby could smell my milk but found the bottle nipple. I did use a preemie nipple for the first several feedings to ensure that the baby had to suck strongly and did not get the milk just flowing out. Sometimes it takes a few tries. Additionally, getting the temperature of the milk just right may be a variable you have to manage. My second boy was much more flexible on the temperature and would take the bottle with room temperature milk. However, my most recent girl is very adamant that her milk be warm. I used trial and error to find what works for us and then stick with it.

As this chapter closes, remember that introducing a bottle is just another step in your broader feeding strategy. It's about making sure that your baby continues to receive the nourishment they need, whether from breast or bottle. You've learned not just when and how to introduce a bottle, but also how to do so in a way that supports your continued breastfeeding. These lessons are part of the larger journey of ensuring your baby thrives from infancy and beyond.

Looking ahead, the next chapter will delve into the complexities and joys of breastfeeding as your baby grows into a toddler. We'll explore how to adapt your breastfeeding techniques as your child becomes more independent, ensuring that this transition is smooth for both of you.

CHAPTER SIX

BREASTFEEDING BEYOND INFANCY

As you watch your little one grow, exploring the world with bright eyes and boundless energy, you may find yourself pondering the continuation of your breastfeeding relationship. Deciding to breastfeed beyond infancy is a path some mothers choose, embracing not only the profound nutritional benefits, but also the deep emotional connection it fosters between mother and child. This chapter delves into the rich tapestry of extended breastfeeding, where nourishment meets nurturing in a dance that spans across various cultures and challenges societal norms. For me, the process of nursing stopped at around one year with both of my boys and was somewhat a process of self weaning. My girl, now five months old, is obviously still breastfeeding and will until she decides it is time to stop, likely around the one-year mark.

6.1 The Benefits of Extended Breastfeeding

Nutritional and Immunological Benefits

Breastfeeding into toddlerhood and beyond continues to offer significant health advantages that extend well into a child's life. Contrary to the common myth that breast milk loses its nutritional value after the first year, it remains a rich source of proteins, fats, vitamins, and minerals—all crucial for your child's development. The composition of breast milk evolves to meet the changing needs of your growing child, providing them with precisely what they need at each stage of development. For instance, the fat and calorie content of breast milk increases as your baby grows, which is essential for the development of their brain and nervous system.

Moreover, the immunological benefits of breast milk continue to shield your child from illnesses and infections. Breast milk is packed with antibodies and immune factors that help fortify your child's immune system. This natural immune boost is particularly beneficial during the toddler years when they begin mingling with other children and are exposed to a myriad of germs. Studies have shown that children who are breastfed beyond infancy experience fewer instances of illnesses such as ear infections, respiratory infections, and gastrointestinal issues. The protective effects of extended breastfeeding in building a robust immune system are backed by extensive research, reinforcing the role of breast milk as more than just food—it's a vital component of your child's health care regimen.

Emotional and Psychological Benefits

The emotional and psychological benefits of extended breastfeeding are profound both for you and your child. It provides a sense of security and comfort to your child, especially during times of stress or change. This secure attachment contributes positively to your child's emotional development, promoting traits like increased independence and self-confidence as they grow.

Breastfeeding beyond infancy also offers mothers a unique way to reconnect with their rapidly growing toddlers, providing quiet moments of closeness in the midst of their active exploration of the world. The oxytocin release stimulated by breastfeeding helps to maintain a nurturing connection, reducing stress and promoting a sense of well-being for you, which in turn helps you engage more positively with your child.

Global Perspectives

Viewing extended breastfeeding through a global lens offers fascinating insights into how different cultures embrace this practice. In many parts of the world, breastfeeding up to two years of age and beyond is common and culturally encouraged. For instance, in Mongolia, children are often breastfed until age three or older, viewed as essential for developing strong, healthy kids. Similarly, in many African and Middle Eastern countries, extended breastfeeding is the norm rather than the exception. These global practices challenge the Western bias towards early weaning and highlight the natural diversity in breastfeeding practices around the world. Embracing a more global perspective helps normalize extended breastfeeding and can empower you to make choices that feel right for your family, free from cultural constraints.

Addressing Common Myths

Let's debunk some myths: Extended breastfeeding does not make your child overly dependent or socially awkward; rather, it fosters independence and confidence by fully meeting their emotional and nutritional needs during crucial developmental years. Another common misconception is that mothers who continue to breastfeed beyond infancy do so solely for their own emotional needs. This couldn't be further from the truth. Extended breastfeeding is a mutual decision that benefits both mother and child in numerous ways, from ensuring optimal health and emotional security for the child to promoting maternal health and strengthening the maternal bond.

As we explore the intricacies and benefits of breastfeeding beyond infancy, remember that your choice to continue breastfeeding is one rooted in a deep understanding of its profound benefits, supported by global practices and scientific research. Each day that you choose to continue is a testament to your commitment to providing the best for your child in a way that respects both cultural wisdom and modern understanding. Embrace this path with confidence and pride, knowing that you are giving your child an invaluable gift that extends well beyond nutrition.

6.2 Dealing with Public Perception and Criticism

Breastfeeding in public is a challenge you will face at some point in your journey. I can remember being in a restaurant in Georgia and my baby waking up and beginning to get fussy. As I would often go to the restroom and occupy a stall to feed, this place only had a single restroom and I did not want to occupy it while others may need it. So we moved to the corner of the restaurant and I faced away from the crowd and discretely allowed my baby to find her meal while covered with her muslin cloth. Sometimes, what you prefer to do is not always an option, so give yourself some grace, do what you need to do and move on. I am positive that some of the people in the restaurant discussed my breastfeeding there, and many probably said they would never do that, however, at that time, on that day, it did not matter to me what others thought.

When you choose to breastfeed beyond infancy, you might find yourself at the center of unsolicited advice and varied opinions. It's not uncommon to face raised eyebrows or outright criticism from those who may not understand your decision. This can come from strangers in public spaces or even from friends and family. Navigating these social challenges requires a blend of confidence in your parenting choices, tactful communication, and sometimes, a strategic choice about when to engage and when to preserve your privacy.

Firstly, standing firm in your decision is crucial. If you find yourself in a situation where you feel comfortable and safe to educate, use it as an opportunity to share insights. You could explain how extended breastfeeding continues to provide vital nutrients and comfort to your child, or share that major health organizations recommend breastfeeding as long as it is mutually desired by mother and child. Sometimes, simply presenting your choice as an informed decision can help others see it in a new light. Sometimes, you will not change minds, but you can validate your choice by sharing that it was well-thought-out.

Balancing the need for privacy with the desire to advocate for extended breastfeeding is a personal decision that can evolve. You might choose to be more open about your breastfeeding relationship in settings where you feel supported and less forthcoming in environments where you anticipate judgment. Both choices are valid. Advocating for acceptance of extended breastfeeding doesn't always mean having public discussions; it can also be about living your truth confidently and allowing others to witness the normalcy and beauty of your choice. By simply being present and visible, you are contributing to a gradual shift in perception and understanding.

6.3 Gentle Weaning Techniques

Weaning is as much a part of the breastfeeding experience as the first latch, yet it often carries a bouquet of mixed emotions and uncertainties. Whether you're considering child-led weaning, where your little one gradually reduces breastfeeding on their own terms, or contemplating a more structured approach initiated by you, the process can be navigated with tenderness and respect for both your needs and those of your child. Both of my boys decided when they wanted to stop nursing organically around the one-year mark. I still mixed some frozen breast milk into their bottle of cow's milk regularly so they continued to get nutritional and immune support. To this day, if my sons get sick, I will mix some breast milk into the milk they are drinking to help them recover faster.

Child-Led Weaning

Child-led weaning is a beautiful, natural process that honors your child's readiness to gradually move away from the breast. This approach relies on your child's cues, gradually decreasing breastfeeding as they show increased interest in other foods and drinks and less interest in nursing. One of the profound benefits of this method is the reduced stress for both you and your child. Since the transition away from breastfeeding is gradual and initiated by your child, it can lead to fewer emotional upheavals. Children often use breastfeeding not just for nutrition but also for comfort and connection. Allowing them to lead the way gives them time to find other forms of comfort and connection, ensuring the change doesn't feel abrupt or unsettling. This method can be particularly effective as your child becomes more engaged in the world, exploring new foods, and enjoying more interactive play, which naturally begins to replace nursing sessions.

Implementing child-led weaning means staying attuned to your child's evolving needs. You might notice they're skipping a usual nursing session in favor of a hearty snack or are too busy playing to pause for a feed. These are signs that they're beginning to wean. During this time, it's beneficial to offer a variety of solid foods and encourage your child to use a cup, which can help them become more accustomed to new ways of eating and drinking. However, be prepared for fluctuations; during times of illness or significant changes, your child might increase breastfeeding for comfort, and that's perfectly okay. It's all part of the ebb and flow of this gentle weaning process.

Mother-Led Weaning Strategies

For mothers initiating weaning, the approach can still be gentle and responsive to your child's needs. Start by identifying the least favorite nursing sessions to eliminate first, usually those during the day when distractions are plentiful. Gradually extending the time between these feedings can help your child adjust slowly. During this time, offer plenty of cuddles and close contact to reassure your child that the physical closeness they associate with breastfeeding is still abundantly available. Introducing new rituals can also be helpful, like a special story time or a cuddle with a favorite book in place of nursing, which can offer comfort and consistency during the transition. It is also ok to eliminate all but one nursing session. I have a close friend who continued to nurse her little boy at bedtime. It was a special time for them and neither her, nor the baby were ready to let go of it by the one-year mark.

Communication Techniques

Open, loving communication is crucial during the weaning process. For toddlers, simple explanations tied to their understanding can be very helpful. Explaining that "milk time" will be shorter because they're growing and can eat more kinds of food helps them make sense of the changes. Using positive language about growing up and becoming big can make the process exciting rather than something they feel they're losing. Always respond to their cues with sensitivity, and reassure them through your actions and words that their needs are being met with love and attention. While they may not be able to communicate fully, talking to your toddler about reducing their "milky-time" will sink in. They understand much more than they can tell you, so talk to them about it.

Emotional Support for Both

Acknowledging the emotional complexities of weaning is vital for both you and your child. It's normal to feel a sense of loss or sadness as this special stage comes to an end, just as it's normal for your child to feel unsettled by the change. Allow yourself to feel these emotions and seek support if needed. Talk about your feelings with friends, your partner, or a support group. For your child, extra cuddles, patience, and reassurance during the weaning process can help them adjust more smoothly. Remember, weaning doesn't mean the end of the close, nurturing relationship you've built with your child; it simply marks the evolution of that relationship. As your relationship evolves, believe me, there will be so many more milestones and fun times that you will be able to replace nursing with. Do not think of it as a loss. Think of it as accomplishing a goal and moving forward to a new set of goals and objectives. I have friends who set a goal of introducing 100 foods to their child or something else related to their nutrition to take up their time. You are a mom, you will not have any free time, haha.

6.4 Maintaining a Bond Beyond Breastfeeding

When the time comes to transition away from breastfeeding, many mothers worry about maintaining that special bond they've nurtured from those first magical moments after birth. It's important to recognize that the end of breastfeeding doesn't mean the end of your deep connection with your child. Instead, it's an opportunity to evolve the relationship and discover new, exciting ways to connect that continue to foster closeness and love. One of the most beautiful aspects of motherhood is watching your relationship with your child grow and change, finding new ways to share love and learning together.

I think of my second son, as soon as I stopped nursing him, he developed a deep attachment and desire to be with his Dad all the time. He now sleeps with Dad and actually prefers him to me, which in the beginning was a bit tough. Nevertheless, I had a full year of time when I was his primary caregiver, so I look at it like it is now his Dad's turn. Seeing the special bond they have developed is so rewarding, not to mention it gives me a little bit of a break.

There are other great ways to bond with your child. Activities like reading books together, doing arts and crafts, or even engaging in a fun cooking project can create wonderful moments of connection. For example, a nightly story time can replace breastfeeding before bed, offering a different but equally soothing routine that helps your child wind down for the night. These moments of closeness reinforce the bond and ensure that your child continues to feel secure and loved. Both of my boys love for me to scratch their back, so they lay across my lap and get a little back scratch often.

It's completely natural to experience feelings of loss or sadness as you transition away from breastfeeding. This change marks the end of a significant phase in your and your baby's life, one that involved intimate moments of nurturing that were uniquely yours to share. It's okay to grieve this change. Reflecting on your breastfeeding experience can be incredibly powerful. Take time to think about what you have done. This reflection can be a source of immense pride and joy. Celebrate the milestones, the quiet moments, the hurdles crossed, and the strength you found along the way.

As your child grows more independent, your role shifts from direct provider to supportive guide. Encouraging independence doesn't mean pulling away; rather, it involves supporting your child's exploration and learning. This can mean letting your child lead in selecting activities or making small decisions. For instance, let them choose which book to read together or what clothes they want to wear. These choices foster a sense of self and confidence in their abilities. As they learn to navigate the world, your support and encouragement will remind them that they always have a safe space to return to.

6.5 Breastfeeding and the Return of Menstruation

When the familiar signs of menstruation return after giving birth, it can bring a mix of relief and anxiety. For many breastfeeding moms, this marks a significant shift not only in their physical health but also in how they manage breastfeeding moving forward. Understanding how your cycle can influence your breastfeeding experience is key to navigating this phase with confidence and ease. When does this occur? The true answer is, it varies. My menstrual cycle did not return until I weaned both of my boys around their first birthday. This timeline can vary and will be different for everyone, so do not be surprised if it is 4 months or 10 months. There is no "normal" timeline for your cycle to return while breastfeeding.

The resumption of your menstrual cycle can sometimes lead to temporary changes in your milk supply and its composition. It's not uncommon to notice a slight dip in milk production in the days leading up to your period, and sometimes during. This is largely due to natural fluctuations in hormone levels, particularly progesterone and estrogen, which can slightly inhibit milk production. Additionally, some mothers report that their breast milk tastes a bit saltier around their period, which might occasionally result in fussiness at the breast. Managing these changes effectively involves maintaining your regular breastfeeding schedule as much as possible, or even increasing the frequency of feedings or pumping sessions to help stimulate production. Staying hydrated and possibly increasing your intake of calcium and magnesium have also been suggested by some studies to help counteract the dip in supply.

With the return of menstruation, fertility also returns, which is an important consideration if you're thinking about expanding your family again. It's a common myth that you can't get pregnant while breastfeeding, but many women experience the return of fertility once their periods resume, even if they are still nursing regularly. This doesn't mean contraception should be an afterthought. If you're not planning another pregnancy soon, discussing contraceptive options that are compatible with breastfeeding is a good idea. This can provide peace of mind, allowing you to focus on your current breastfeeding journey and family dynamics without the immediate surprise of another pregnancy.

Looking ahead, the next chapter will delve into the practical aspects of balancing breastfeeding with the realities of returning to work. This transition poses its own set of challenges and learning curves, and being prepared can make all the difference in continuing your breastfeeding journey successfully.

CHAPTER SEVEN

PUMPING AND STORING BREASTMILK

Navigating the world of breast pumps and bottle feeding can feel a bit like stepping into a bustling market, where every stall shouts the virtues of its wares, leaving you wondering which one truly fits your needs. Whether you're returning to work, planning a night out, or simply need a break, finding the right tools to continue providing breast milk to your baby is crucial. This chapter is your friendly guide through the bustling market of breast pumps and bottle feeding, helping you make choices that feel right for you and your baby.

One of the first questions I had when returning to work was how much breastmilk do I need in the freezer to stop pumping. The answer to this question is not always simple. Your newborn baby drinks less than your 6-month-old baby, obviously, but your 6-month-old is starting solids, so what is the real number of ounces of breastmilk needed. I did a great deal of research and came up with my idea of what I needed. I base my storage needs on the idea that, on average, an infant needs approximately 25 ounces of breastmilk daily, so at first glance, it is safe to say that 9,125 ounces is what you need for your baby's first year. In my breastfeeding world, for the first 6 weeks, I was nursing and pumping and adding about 25 ounces to my freezer stash daily. So then, I went down the rabbit hole of only needing to feed my baby during the day as I am at home at night and handle feedings during that time by nursing. Then I began to think about the idea that I do not use any of my stored milk on the weekend either. As you can see, I am trying to get to a point where I no longer need to pump. What I came up with is 750 ounces per month is the most milk you should need, that is 25 ounces daily, which you likely will not use if you are nursing some of the day, but is a good gauge to use for planning.

Overall, pumping for away time or exclusively pumping takes a great deal of organization and planning. One of the common issues moms often encounter is the feeling that they are not making enough and want to increase their supply. I have included a chart below to give you some guidance on how to increase, decrease or maintain supply. Please remember that every breastfeeding experience is different. You may be an undersupply, oversupplier or supply exactly what is needed. All of those scenarios are sufficient. Myself, I have historically experienced good supply and can pump just twice daily and maintain my supply. Some moms may require pumping 4-5 times to maintain supply. Listen to your body and see how it responds to what you are doing and make decisions based on the info(and milk) that you have. The guidance below is just that... GUIDANCE.

Breast Pumping Chart for Maintaining, Increasing, or Decreasing Milk Supply

Goal	Frequency (Times per Day)	Duration per Session	Total Ounces per Day	Notes
Maintain Supply	8-12 times (every 2-3 hours)	15-20 minutes	25-35 ounces	Pump or nurse every 2-3 hours, including nighttime sessions. Ensure consistent output by emptying breasts completely.
Increase Supply	10-12 times (every 2 hours)	20-30 minutes	No specific amount; focus on frequency	Power pumping once a day can help (pump 10 min, rest 10 min for 1 hour). The more stimulation, the more milk will be produced.
Decrease Supply	4-6 times (every 4-6 hours)	10-15 minutes	Gradually decrease by 2-4 ounces per day	Gradually reduce pumping or nursing sessions. Pump or nurse just enough to relieve fullness, reducing stimulation to signal a drop in milk production.

7.1 Choosing the Right Breast Pump for Your Needs

Identifying Your Pumping Needs

Understanding your lifestyle and breastfeeding goals is the first step in choosing a breast pump that fits seamlessly into your daily routine. Are you a full-time working mom who needs to pump several times a day at work? Or are you a stay-at-home mom who might only need to pump occasionally to have a bottle ready for outings or appointments? Perhaps you're planning to exclusively pump, requiring a robust solution that can handle frequent use. Assessing how often, where, and why you'll need to pump will guide your decision-making process. Consider also how much time you can dedicate to pumping; if time is limited, a fast and efficient pump might be at the top of your list.

Types of Breast Pumps

There's a variety of breast pumps available, each with its own set of pros and cons. Manual pumps are lightweight, portable, and relatively inexpensive. They're ideal for moms who pump occasionally and don't want to worry about batteries or power sources. However, manual pumping requires more physical effort and time, which might not be ideal for regular use. Electric pumps, on the other hand, are faster and more efficient, making them suitable for daily use, especially for moms returning to work. They do tend to be pricier and less portable than manual pumps, though many models are now designed to be more travel-friendly. Battery-operated pumps offer a good middle ground, providing the convenience of an electric pump without the need for a power outlet, though the cost of replacing batteries can add up. Additionally, there are tools like the haaka that can assist with milk collection as you navigate pumping and storing your milk.

Important Features to Consider

When choosing a breast pump, several features can make your pumping experience smoother and more comfortable. Adjustable suction levels allow you to control the pumping intensity, making the process more comfortable and potentially more efficient. Look for a pump that mimics the natural rhythm of a nursing baby, with a phase for stimulation (to start the milk flow) followed by a deeper suction phase. Double pumping capability, which allows you to pump both breasts simultaneously, can be a great time-saver and may also help increase your milk supply. Noise level is another consideration; a quieter pump can be less disruptive, especially if you need to pump at work or while your baby is sleeping.

Seeking Recommendations and Reviews

With so many options on the market, tapping into the experiences of other mothers can be incredibly valuable. Ask for recommendations from friends who have been through similar pumping needs. Lactation consultants can also provide professional advice based on your specific circumstances. They might recommend a particular type of pump that aligns with your breastfeeding goals and challenges. Additionally, online reviews can be a goldmine of information, offering insights into the durability, efficiency, and ease of use of different pumps. Remember, what works for one mother might not work for another, so gather a range of opinions and weigh them against your personal needs and preferences.

TIP: So I have not put this tip into place, as I am almost to the end of my breastfeeding journey, but if I had it to do over again, I would have gotten one pump to keep and work and one to have at home. When you return to work, remembering to get the pump every day and take it back and forth has been really difficult and inconvenient. If you have the financial capability to get two pumps, do it. You will not regret keeping one at work. Many times, I have had to come back to my office at night or go home during the day, because I forgot to get my pump or pump parts. You may even be able to find a less expensive or used option that could suffice for work depending on how much pumping you are going to need to do.

7.2 Mastering Efficient Pumping Routines

Establishing a regular pumping routine that closely mirrors your baby's natural feeding schedule can significantly ease the transition to pumping, whether you're at home, work, or even on the go. Ideally, you'll want to pump around the same times your baby usually feeds, which helps maintain your milk supply by keeping the demand consistent. This might mean pumping every few hours, and while it sounds daunting, having a set schedule can actually simplify your day, helping you plan around these essential breaks. For mothers returning to work, starting this routine a few weeks beforehand can also help ease any anxieties about maintaining supply. As previously mentioned, I began pumping to relieve engorgement nearly immediately when my babies were born, so my body was used to the process. It's all about creating a rhythm that feels as natural as possible, mimicking the usual breastfeeding routine you and your baby have grown accustomed to.

Keeping your pumping equipment clean and well-maintained is non-negotiable. Every part of your breast pump that comes into contact with your milk should be thoroughly washed after each use. This prevents the build-up of bacteria and ensures your milk stays as clean and safe as possible for your baby. Use hot, soapy water or a dishwasher if the components are dishwasher-safe. Allow everything to air dry on a clean towel to prevent contamination from clothes. Regular checks for any parts that might need replacement, such as the tubing or membranes, ensure your pump remains effective and hygienic. This routine might seem time-consuming initially, but it becomes second nature rapidly, much like washing bottles or preparing your baby's bath. One tip here is that you can place your pump parts in a zip-lock bag and into the refrigerator if you will be pumping often.

Navigating pumping at work requires a blend of preparation and communication. Before returning to work, discuss your needs with your employer to ensure there's a private and comfortable space for pumping. Federal law requires employers to provide reasonable break times and a private space (not a bathroom) for mothers to express milk for up to one year after the child's birth. Planning your pumping times around your usual work schedule can help minimize stress. For example, scheduling sessions during usual break times or in between meetings can make it easier to manage. Remember, maintaining flexibility is key, as some days might require adjusting times based on your workload or meetings. Keeping an insulated storage bag at work for your expressed milk ensures it remains fresh until you can get it home to your baby, making your workday pumping routine efficient and stress-free.

In addition to figuring out the schedules for pumping, you need to be prepared for the mishaps. I highly recommend keeping a change of clothes in your car and additional milk absorbing pads too. Just recently, I was at a meeting out of town and went to my car to pump. Something went wrong and I leaked breast milk all over the clothes I had on, causing me to have to leave the meeting and miss the second half of the training. Have extra clothes. One would think I would have already thought of this, but in my mind, I was an experienced pumper so would not have an issue. I now have a set of business and casual clothes in my car, just in case.

7.3 Safe Storage Practices for Breastmilk

Storing breast milk safely is like preserving a precious food source that offers immense benefits to your baby when you're not around to breastfeed directly. It's crucial to handle this valuable nutrition with care to ensure it retains its quality and safety. When you've taken the time to pump, knowing how to store your milk properly can make all the difference in your baby's feeding experience. Let's dive into the essentials of storing breast milk, focusing on maintaining its freshness and nutritional value.

Firstly, understanding and following storage guidelines is paramount. Freshly expressed breast milk can be kept at room temperature (up to 77°F or 25°C) for about four to six hours, though it's always safest to store it in a cooler or refrigerator as soon as possible. If you're at work or on the move, using an insulated cooler with ice packs can keep the milk safe for up to 24 hours. For longer storage, the refrigerator is your ally. Store breast milk in the back, where the temperature is most consistent, for up to four days. If you won't be using the refrigerated milk within four days, freezing it is a great option. In a standard freezer compartment of a refrigerator, it can be safely stored for two weeks, but in a standalone deep freezer at a constant 0°F (-18°C), it can last up to 12 months, though using it within six months is optimal for preserving the best quality. While it is a little less than what is safe, I tried to operate on 4s.

Here is your milk storage quick guide:

- Fresh Milk: 4 hours at room temperature or 4 days in the refrigerator

- Frozen Milk: two weeks if kept in the inside freezer or up to 12 months in a deep freezer.

Choosing the right containers for storing breast milk is another critical decision. While there are various options, each has its pros and cons depending on your needs. Breast milk storage bags, specifically designed for this purpose, are popular for their convenience and space-saving qualities in the freezer. These bags are pre-sterilized, durable, and designed to protect the milk from contamination and freezer burn. However, if you're looking for a reusable option, glass or BPA-free plastic bottles can be excellent choices. Glass bottles are the most inert option that won't interact chemically with breast milk, ensuring no substances leach into your milk. They are also sustainable but need careful handling to avoid breakage. BPA-free plastic bottles or containers offer a lightweight and unbreakable alternative but ensure they are specifically meant for breast milk storage to avoid any chemical leaching.

Labeling and organizing your milk effectively can save you a lot of hassle and ensure the milk is used in the best condition. Always label each container with the date the milk was expressed. If you're adding fresh milk to frozen milk, cool it in the refrigerator first to prevent thawing of the frozen portion. Organize the storage space so that the oldest milk is used first, following the "first in, first out" principle. This practice helps in minimizing waste and providing your baby with the best quality milk at all times.

Thawing and warming breast milk correctly is as important as how it is stored. Always thaw the oldest milk first — the milk that was pumped the earliest. Thaw it in the refrigerator overnight or by holding the container under warm running water. Avoid using a microwave to thaw or heat breast milk, as it can create hot spots that might scald your baby's mouth and destroy some of the beneficial milk components. Once the milk is thawed, gently swirl the container to mix any fat that has separated (never shake vigorously, as it can break down some of the milk's proteins). Warm the milk to body temperature by placing the container in a bowl of warm water for a few minutes before testing the milk temperature by sprinkling a few drops on your wrist. It should feel warm, not hot.

Implementing these storage practices ensures that every bottle you prepare from your stored milk is as nourishing and safe as the last. This careful attention to detail in storing breast milk means your baby continues to receive the best nutrition possible, even when you're apart. It allows you to maintain a supply of breast milk that's ready whenever your baby needs it, providing peace of mind that you're giving your baby the best start in life, no matter your schedule.

For freezer storage, I have started using the brick method. That means freezing milk bags flat, then once you get 10, putting them in a gallon zip-lock bag in the form of a brick. It should help with conserving space in your freezer instead of having loose bags of milk going everywhere. In the early days, I put smaller amounts in my milk bags so that it would not be wasted as I went back to work after 6 weeks. Since that time, I have been freezing 5 ounce bags, 10 per brick. So you can count your bricks and know how much milk you have. This method also makes it easier to make sure you are using your milk on a first in, first out basis, as you can write on the outside of the gallon bag the dates that are inside.

Another, newer storage technique that I have not used, but have heard of is freeze drying the breastmilk to be used like formula as your very own breast milk powder that can be mixed with water. While this concept is not new, the popularity seems to be growing as more people are using freeze drying as a side-gig. I would definitely speak to your pediatrician about this idea to ensure the safety of the process for your baby to ingest.

7.4 Supplementing with Formula

Breastfeeding is widely celebrated for its numerous benefits to both mother and baby, but there are times when supplementing with formula becomes a practical choice. Whether due to a low milk supply, a demanding schedule, or other reasons, many parents find themselves considering how to combine breastmilk with formula. This chapter explores how to effectively supplement breastfeeding with formula, including tips on mixing breastmilk with formula and advice for managing both feeding methods.

Combining breastmilk and formula can offer flexibility and peace of mind, especially for mothers returning to work or facing challenges with milk production. It allows for the benefits of breastfeeding—such as the transfer of essential antibodies and a unique bond with the baby—while also ensuring the baby gets enough nutrition. For many families, this blended approach can ease stress and provide a balanced feeding strategy. Before introducing formulas, it's essential to consider why supplementation might be necessary. Common reasons include:

- Low Milk Supply: Some mothers may have difficulty producing enough milk, making formula an essential supplement.

- Returning to Work: For working mothers, formula can be a practical solution for times when breastfeeding isn't possible.

- Health Concerns: Sometimes, health issues for the mother or baby necessitate supplementing.

- Convenience and Flexibility: Formula can provide flexibility in feeding schedules and allow other caregivers to help with feedings.

Mixing Formula with Breastmilk

When it comes to combining breastmilk with formula, many parents find it helpful to mix the two. This can be particularly useful for easing the baby into formula while still providing the benefits of breastmilk. Here's how to do it:

1. Prepare Formula and Breastmilk Separately: Always prepare formula according to the manufacturer's instructions and store it properly. Breastmilk should be expressed and stored using safe practices. Never mix formula with thawed breast milk directly.

2. Combine at Feeding Time: If you're mixing for a single feeding, you can combine breastmilk and formula in the same bottle. This approach can be helpful if your baby is reluctant to take formula alone. Ensure that the formula and breastmilk are both at the correct temperature before mixing.

3. Gradual Mixing: Start by adding a small amount of formula to the breast milk. Gradually increase the ratio of formula to breastmilk over time, which can help your baby adjust to the taste and texture of formula.

4. Storage and Handling: If you prepare a mixture in advance, use it within 24 hours and store it in the refrigerator. Never freeze breastmilk that has been mixed with formula.

Remember, every family's situation is unique, so what works best will depend on your specific needs and circumstances. Adding formula to your feeding strategy can extend your freezer stash of breastmilk that may begin dwindling as you return to work or allow for you to provide more substantial calories to your baby's diet. My second born digested breast milk so quickly and as he became more active, we used a small amount of formula to supplement the calories he was getting from breast milk. Always seek support from healthcare professionals and trusted advisors to ensure the best outcomes for both you and your baby.

CHAPTER EIGHT

SPECIAL CONSIDERATIONS

Navigating the breastfeeding landscape while juggling other aspects of your life can sometimes feel like you're trying to solve a complex puzzle. Each piece represents a different part of your daily routine, and figuring out how they all fit together to support your breastfeeding goals adds another layer of challenge. This chapter focuses on those who are balancing a full-time job while continuing to breastfeed.

8.1 Breastfeeding with a Full-time Job: Your Rights and Schedule

Understanding Your Rights

First things first, let's talk about your rights because knowing them is the first step in advocating for yourself and your baby in the workplace. In the United States, the "Break Time for Nursing Mothers" law requires employers to provide reasonable break time for an employee to express breast milk for her nursing child for one year after the child's birth. Employers must also provide a place, other than a bathroom, that is shielded from view and free from intrusion from coworkers and the public. This might sound pretty straightforward, but the reality can vary depending on your workplace environment and its culture. It's helpful to review your company's policies on breastfeeding and pumping. If there isn't a clear policy in place, don't worry, you're paving the way for future nursing mothers in your company. Approach your HR department to discuss your needs; this can also help clarify any points and ensure you're supported.

Planning Your Return to Work

Returning to work post-birth involves more than just setting an alarm and packing your lunch; it requires careful planning, especially when you're breastfeeding. Start by introducing a breast pump to your routine a few weeks before you return to work. This helps build a stash of milk to ensure your baby has enough while you're away and gets you accustomed to pumping, making it less of a hurdle later on. Consider doing a trial run a week or so before your official start date. This could involve pumping at times you would at work and having someone else bottle-feed your baby. These dry runs can help smooth out any kinks in your planned schedule and make the transition easier for both you and your baby. It is often difficult to make the time to pump at work. If you are like me, I found myself stretching my pumping time further and further as I returned to work with all three of my children, causing my milk supply to slow down. I had to make a concerted effort to maintain supply and get my work done.

Communicating with Employers

Open communication with your employer is key to a smooth transition back to work. When discussing your breastfeeding needs, be clear about the specifics—how often you'll need breaks and a suitable area to pump. It's not just about logistics; it's about fostering understanding. If possible, provide solutions that align with your work schedule, like aligning your pumping times with regular break times or offering to come in earlier or stay later to make up the time. Remember, the goal is to find a balance that respects both your needs as a breastfeeding mother and the operational needs of your employer.

Balancing Work and Pumping

Finding that sweet spot where work and pumping schedules align harmoniously is crucial. You might need to pump every few hours, so look at your work schedule and identify times that align with your natural breaks—mid-morning, lunchtime, and mid-afternoon are common options. Keep a pumping log to track when and how much you pump; this can help you adjust your schedule if needed based on your output and your baby's needs. Also, invest in a good-quality, portable breast pump that's efficient and quiet—this makes a world of difference in a workplace setting. Keeping an extra set of pumping gear at work can save you from potential stress if you forget something at home.

My pumping activities included an early morning pump before work that held me over until lunchtime when I would pump. After that, I waited until I got home to either pump or nurse, depending on my baby's schedule. With this schedule, I was only pumping once at work, but it took several weeks to get to that schedule. Remember, your needs are going to vary depending on your body, your baby's needs and your work schedule. Be flexible and determine what works for you and go with it.

Visual Element: Pumping Schedule Template

It is often helpful to create a template and visual aid to ensure you are meeting your pumping needs. Print it out and get a copy of it to your supervisor and keep a copy at your workstation. Below are the two schedules I have used with my children.

WORKDAY PUMPING SCHEDULE (Weeks 6-12)

6 AM- At home pump (Approximately 12 oz)

11 AM- At work pump (Approximately 8 oz)

4 PM- At work pump (Approximately 6 oz)

WORKDAY PUMPING SCHEDULE (Weeks 12-26)

6 AM- At home pump (Approximately 12 oz)

12:30 PM- At work pump (Approximately 8 oz)

This template is just a starting point. There are various ways to plan your pumping sessions. You may want to pump more if you have a daily milk amount you need to put into the freezer. If you are doing the pitcher method and using today's milk for tomorrow, then you know how much you need and will need to adjust the schedule to meet those needs. Each day might look a little different, and that's perfectly okay, but consistency will make planning and preparation much easier as you settle into somewhat of a routine.

8.2 Breastfeeding Premature Babies: Special Considerations

When your little one arrives earlier than expected, the world of breast-feeding can feel even more daunting. Premature babies often face a unique set of challenges that can make the natural act of breastfeeding seem like a steep mountain to climb. However, with the right support and techniques, you can make significant strides in providing your preemie with the best start, despite the hurdles you both might face. Even if your baby is not a preemie, but has a low birth weight, you may face similar challenges to preemies like the need for frequent feedings to ensure sugar levels stay within the normal range. My last child was born at 5 lbs, 7 ounces, then dropped to 5 lbs 1 oz. Early on, she had a little trouble regulating her sugar, which required more frequent feedings than normal to ensure that her sugar was staying up. Whatever you encounter, analyze, adjust and move forward. This process is flexible and ever-changing.

Challenges and Solutions

Premature babies typically have less energy for feeds and might struggle with latch-on due to their smaller, less developed oral structures. This can lead to difficulties in extracting milk, which might initially discourage you. But here's where your persistence and patience shine. Working closely with a lactation consultant can provide you with targeted techniques and positions to help your baby latch more effectively. Sometimes, using a nipple shield under professional guidance can help your baby latch on to the breast, as it can make the nipple more pronounced and easier for your tiny one to grasp. The key here is consistency and trying different approaches under professional supervision until you find what works best for your baby.

Breast milk is incredibly important for premature babies, not just for nutrition, but also for its protective properties against infections and diseases, which preemies are particularly vulnerable to. Since their nutritional needs are higher, and their ability to breastfeed might be compromised, expressing milk becomes a crucial part of the breastfeeding process. This ensures they still receive your milk even if direct breastfeeding isn't possible initially.

Kangaroo Care

The power of skin-to-skin contact, or Kangaroo Care, cannot be overstated, especially for premature babies. This practice involves holding your baby against your skin, which can greatly aid in stabilizing their heart rate, breathing, and temperature. But the benefits extend to breastfeeding as well. Kangaroo Care can enhance your baby's instinct to breastfeed and has been shown to improve milk production. It fosters a unique bond and provides a comforting environment that can make the transition to breastfeeding smoother. Integrate Kangaroo Care into your routine as often as you can, making it a peaceful time for both you and your baby to connect and relax together.

Expressing Milk for Premature Babies

Expressing milk is often a necessity for mothers of premature babies. In the early days, your baby might not be strong enough to breastfeed directly, or they might need to stay in the NICU where direct access might be limited. Using a hospital-grade pump can help you establish and maintain your milk supply during this time. These pumps are designed to mimic a baby's natural sucking pattern, which is crucial for stimulating your milk production effectively. Start pumping as soon as you can after delivery, ideally within the first six hours if possible. Establishing a regular pumping schedule, about every three hours around the clock, can help mimic your baby's natural feeding times and support your milk supply. While the hospital does have a pump, I was more comfortable bringing my pump from home and using it.

Collaborating with Healthcare Providers

Your collaboration with neonatologists, nurses, and lactation consultants in the NICU is vital. These professionals are your allies, equipped with the knowledge and experience to support you through the breastfeeding process. They can offer hands-on assistance with latching, guidance on using breast pumps, and continuous support for any breastfeeding issues that arise. Their expertise can be invaluable in helping you navigate the often complex and emotional process of breastfeeding a premature baby. Regular discussions and updates with your healthcare team can help you stay informed about your baby's progress and any adjustments needed in your breastfeeding strategy.

8.3 Breastfeeding Multiples: Strategies for Success

When you find out you're expecting multiples, the joy is often twofold or more, but so, potentially, are the concerns—especially when it comes to breastfeeding. Feeding two or more babies can sound daunting, but with some strategic planning and the right support, you can navigate this beautifully chaotic experience with confidence. Let's unpack some approaches and tips that can help you whether you choose to feed your babies simultaneously or sequentially.

Simultaneous feeding, where you nurse more than one baby at a time, has its perks. It can be a real time-saver, allowing you to maintain a more streamlined feeding schedule. Imagine having twins; breastfeeding them together means the feeding sessions finish at the same time, freeing up your time for other tasks or much-needed rest. However, it requires a bit of coordination and practice to get comfortable. Using a twin nursing pillow can be a game-changer here. These pillows are designed to support multiple babies comfortably, helping you position each baby at the breast without feeling like you need an extra set of hands.

On the other hand, sequential feeding, where you nurse one baby at a time, allows for individual bonding with each baby and can be simpler logistically when you're just starting out. This approach lets you adjust your position and technique to each baby's unique preferences and needs, which can be particularly beneficial if one of your babies has more difficulty latching or needs more attention during feeds. The downside is that it can be time-consuming, as you spend double or triple the time feeding. But remember, there's no right or wrong choice here—what matters is finding what works best for you and your babies.

Remember, feeding multiples is a marathon, not a sprint. It takes patience, perseverance, and a lot of trial and error to find what works best for you and your babies. Each day might bring new challenges, but also new moments of joy and accomplishment. As you adapt and learn, you'll not only become more proficient at meeting your babies' needs, but you'll also strengthen the bonds that hold your growing family together.

8.4 Introducing a Pacifier... or Not

The decision to introduce a pacifier to your baby is a personal one and can depend on a variety of factors. Pacifiers can offer benefits, but they also come with potential drawbacks. This section explores the advantages and disadvantages of pacifier use, along with additional considerations to help you make an informed decision.

Advantages of Using a Pacifier

- Soothing Effect: Pacifiers can help calm a fussy baby and provide comfort, especially during stressful situations like teething or vaccinations. Often, breastfeeding moms end up being human pacifiers, so this offers an alternative soothing technique for your baby.

- SIDS Risk Reduction: Some studies suggest that pacifier use during sleep may reduce the risk of sudden infant death syndrome (SIDS). The exact reason is unclear, but it is a commonly cited benefit.

- Non-Nutritive Sucking: Pacifiers satisfy the baby's need to suck, which can be soothing and provide a sense of security without needing to nurse or bottle-feed. Pacifiers can help some babies fall asleep more easily and stay asleep longer, which can be beneficial for both the baby and the parents.

Disadvantages of Using a Pacifier

- Nipple Confusion: Introducing a pacifier too early can lead to nipple confusion, where the baby may have difficulty latching onto the breast properly. This is particularly a concern in the first few weeks of breastfeeding.

- Dental Issues: Prolonged pacifier use can lead to dental problems, such as misaligned teeth or changes in the shape of the mouth. It's generally recommended to wean off the pacifier by age 2.

- Dependence: Some babies may become overly dependent on the pacifier to fall asleep or soothe themselves, making it challenging to wean off later.

- Ear Infections: There is some evidence suggesting that pacifier use may increase the risk of ear infections, although this risk is relatively small.

When considering introducing a pacifier, several additional factors should be taken into account. Timing is important; many experts suggest waiting until breastfeeding is well established, typically around 3-4 weeks, to avoid potential breastfeeding issues. Choosing the right type of pacifier is also crucial; opt for one that is orthodontically designed to reduce the risk of dental problems, is BPA-free, and has a shield that is larger than the baby's mouth to prevent choking hazards. Regular hygiene practices are essential, so clean and sterilize pacifiers frequently to prevent infections and replace them periodically to avoid wear and tear. Your parenting style should also influence your decision; some parents find pacifiers beneficial, while others prefer alternative soothing techniques such as rocking or gentle shushing. Additionally, consider your family's health history; if there are concerns about dental health or ear infections, discuss them with your pediatrician before introducing a pacifier. Finally, if you choose to use a pacifier, plan for a gradual weaning process to minimize stress and allow your baby to adapt to other soothing methods.

Ultimately, the decision to introduce a pacifier should be based on your baby's needs and your family's preferences. To make an informed choice, start by evaluating whether your baby seems to need extra soothing or comfort and if a pacifier might help address those needs. Be prepared to adapt your approach based on your baby's response to the pacifier and make adjustments as needed.

8.5 Donor Milk: Understanding Your Options

When breastfeeding directly might not be an option, especially in cases involving premature or ill infants, donor milk represents a possible alternative that provides the necessary nutritional and immune-boosting benefits to help babies thrive. The concept of using donor milk hinges on its close composition to mother's milk, containing a balance of nutrients, enzymes, and antibodies uniquely suited to human infants.

When considering donor milk, finding a reputable milk bank is the first step. Milk banks screen their donors rigorously to ensure safety and handle the milk with meticulous care. The Human Milk Banking Association of North America (HMBANA) sets high standards for processing human milk, which includes pasteurizing the milk to eliminate any viruses or bacteria while preserving its valuable components. These banks also prioritize distributing milk based on medical necessity, with premature and sick babies at the top of the list. To find a milk bank, you can start by visiting the HMBANA website or consulting with your hospital's neonatal unit, which often has connections with national or regional milk banks.

However, not everyone has access to milk banks, and some might turn to more informal milk-sharing arrangements. While sharing breast milk informally among friends or through community networks can seem like a good solution, it's vital to proceed with caution. Unlike milk from certified banks, informally shared milk hasn't been screened or pasteurized, presenting potential risks such as the transmission of diseases or exposure to medications and drugs taken by the donor. If considering this route, it's crucial to thoroughly screen donors and ideally, have the milk pasteurized, though this can be complex and not always feasible.

The cost and accessibility of donor milk can also be a significant consideration. Milk from certified banks often comes with a price that includes processing and handling, which can be costly. Some insurance plans might cover these costs, but this is not always the case. It's advisable to check with your insurance provider and also explore financial aid options that some milk banks offer to families in need. These programs can help offset the costs, making donor milk a more accessible option for those who need it most. If you intend to use a more informal approach, it may be possible to assist your donor in other ways besides financial compensation. I have friends who have shared milk with others at no cost just because they want to.

As we close this chapter on special situations, the underlying theme has been about finding solutions that work for you and your baby. Each section has provided strategies to manage these unique situations, ensuring that you feel empowered and informed no matter what your breastfeeding journey looks like. As we move forward, the next chapter will delve into additional uses for breastmilk and it's great healing properties.

CHAPTER NINE

THE HEALING POWER OF BREAST MILK

Motherhood brings with it a toolkit filled with more than just bottles and bibs; it comes with the incredible, almost mystical properties of breast milk. Often celebrated primarily for its nutritional value, breast milk also harbors a host of natural healing properties that can soothe, protect, and heal your baby in ways you might not have imagined. In this chapter, we'll explore how this extraordinary substance can be your ally not just in nourishment, but also in natural healthcare.

9.1 Natural Remedies: Breast Milk for Baby's Ailments

Breast milk is not only food but medicine too, a marvel of nature that's readily available, completely tailored to your baby, and packed with antibacterial properties. These properties make breast milk a potent tool for treating minor cuts and scrapes your baby might encounter. It contains a component called lactoferrin, which provides antibacterial, antiviral, and anti-inflammatory benefits. This means a few drops of breast milk applied to a minor scrape or cut can help prevent infection naturally.

Moving beyond cuts and scrapes, breast milk is a soothing agent for various skin conditions that commonly distress babies, such as diaper rash or eczema. Its natural moisturizers and healing compounds can soothe irritated skin gently and effectively. For diaper rash, after a diaper change, you can apply a few drops of breast milk to the affected area before putting on a fresh diaper. Its healing touch can help reduce redness and soothe discomfort without the need for commercial creams or ointments. For eczema, which can make your baby's skin dry and itchy, applying breast milk can help hydrate and calm the skin, offering relief that's both gentle and free from chemicals.

Eye infections, like blocked tear ducts or conjunctivitis, can also be alleviated with a few drops of breast milk. The antibacterial properties can help clear up the infection, reducing redness and discharge naturally. Simply cleanse your baby's eye with a sterile cotton pad, and gently apply a few drops of breast milk directly to the surface of the eye or inside the lower eyelid. Many parents find this method a comforting alternative to prescription treatments, often noting improvement within a few days. In my baby's early days, she had a great deal of eye matter every morning for several days, until I began applying breast milk directly to her eye.

Lastly, the benefits of breastfeeding extend to times when your baby might be battling colds or the flu. Breast milk isn't just a source of hydration; it's packed with immune-boosting antibodies that can help your baby fight off viruses more effectively. Nursing also provides comfort that can be especially soothing when your baby feels unwell. The act of breastfeeding can help clear nasal congestion and promote better breathing, which is particularly helpful when little noses are stuffed up. Breastmilk can be used in the nose, just a few drops at a time to help with congestion.

9.2 Breast Milk and Infant Allergies: What the Research Says

Studies suggest that the natural components found in breast milk can help to regulate the development of the immune system. This regulation helps the baby's body learn to differentiate between harmful pathogens and non-harmful antigens, such as food proteins, reducing the likelihood of allergic reactions. Moreover, the unique antibodies in breast milk, tailored specifically to the mother's environment, provide a form of early immune training. This training strengthens the baby's own immune responses, making them more adept at handling potential allergens as they grow.

The World Health Organization (WHO) underscores the importance of exclusive breastfeeding for the first six months of life as a strategy to bolster this protective effect against allergies. Exclusive breastfeeding during this time provides continuous immune support and allows the infant's digestive system to mature adequately. The digestive system plays a crucial role in how the body handles potential allergens, and a well-developed system can better manage and process these substances, reducing the risk of allergies.

As your baby grows and you start thinking about introducing solid foods, the timing and choice of these foods can also influence allergy development. Recent guidelines have shifted the perspective on when to introduce allergenic foods such as peanuts, eggs, and dairy. It was once thought that delaying the introduction of these foods could help prevent allergies. However, recent findings suggest the opposite may be true—introducing allergenic foods while continuing to breastfeed can actually help reduce the risk of developing food allergies. This approach allows your baby's immune system to learn to tolerate these allergens early on, particularly when supported by the protective effects of breast milk.

Navigating the landscape of breastfeeding and its impact on allergies is a vivid reminder of how interconnected our bodies and our diets are with the environment we live in. As research continues to evolve, so too does our understanding of how best to use breastfeeding not just to feed but to protect our children.

9.3 DIY Breast Milk Lotions

Breast milk's versatility extends beyond feeding; it's also a wonderful ingredient for homemade skincare products. Imagine turning this natural elixir into gentle soaps, soothing lotions, and healing balms that benefit not only your baby but also you. These homemade remedies utilize the natural properties of breast milk and are especially suited for sensitive skin, providing a safe and effective way to care for your family's skincare needs.

Starting with a simple breast milk soap, this is a delightful way to gently cleanse your baby's delicate skin or even your own. To create this soap, you'll need about 2 ounces of fresh breast milk, 2 ounces of distilled water, 3.5 ounces of lye (sodium hydroxide), and 12 ounces of coconut oil. First, ensure you're working in a well-ventilated area and wearing protective gloves and eyewear. Slowly add the lye to the water (never the other way around), stirring constantly until fully dissolved; the solution will heat up and emit fumes, which is normal. Allow this mixture to cool. Gently warm the coconut oil until it melts, then combine it with the cooled lye solution. Slowly add your breast milk while blending with a stick blender until the mixture reaches a light trace (similar to thin pudding). Pour into molds and cover lightly with wax paper, then wrap in towels to insulate. After

24 hours, unmold and cut the soap into bars. Cure these bars on a rack for about four weeks before using. This soap not only cleanses but also benefits from the moisturizing and soothing properties of breast milk, making it perfect for eczema-prone or sensitive skin.

Next, let's talk about a homemade breast milk lotion, ideal for moisturizing and healing dry skin or irritation. For this lotion, you'll need a quarter cup of breast milk, a quarter cup of distilled water, a quarter cup of an oil of your choice (like almond or olive oil), and a tablespoon of beeswax. Start by gently melting the beeswax with the oil in a double boiler. In another pot, warm the breast milk with the water—do not boil. Once the beeswax and oil are melted and combined, slowly add the warm milk mixture while stirring vigorously. As it cools, continue to stir; you may use a hand mixer for a smoother consistency. Once fully cooled, transfer the lotion into a clean jar. This lotion harnesses the hydrating properties of the oils and the healing effects of breast milk, making it a fantastic remedy for dry patches or diaper rashes.

For those times when you or your baby might experience nipple soreness or severe diaper rash, a breast milk healing balm can be a lifesaver. To make this, you'll need two tablespoons of breast milk, one tablespoon of coconut oil, one tablespoon of shea butter, and one tablespoon of beeswax. Melt the shea butter, coconut oil, and beeswax together in a double boiler. Remove from heat and allow to cool slightly before whisking in the breast milk until you achieve a uniform consistency. Pour the mixture into a small container and allow it to set. This balm uses the natural soothing and anti-inflammatory properties of breast milk, combined with the moisturizing benefits of shea butter and coconut oil, to create a potent remedy for sore or chapped skin.

Storing these homemade products correctly is crucial to maintaining their effectiveness and safety. Since these products contain fresh breast milk, their shelf life is shorter than commercial products. Store them in a cool, dark place and use them within a week. For longer storage, refrigeration can extend their usability up to two weeks. Always check for any signs of spoilage before use, as the freshness of the ingredients directly impacts the product's safety and effectiveness. The first time I made these, I reduced the recipe by half to make sure I did not waste any of the soap or lotion. There are also various other sources of recipes for soaps, lotions and other balms

Reflecting on Immunity and Breast Milk

As we close this exploration of the immunological benefits of breast milk, it's clear that its value extends far beyond basic nutrition. Breast milk is a dynamic, responsive substance that plays a critical role in shaping your baby's immune landscape. It offers immediate protective benefits against infections and sets the stage for long-term health advantages. As we transition to the next chapter, we will look at self-care for mom.

CHAPTER TEN

SELF-CARE AND EMOTIONAL WELLNESS FOR THE BREASTFEEDING MOM

10.1 Finding Your Breastfeeding Support Network

The importance of having a robust support system while you navigate the complexities of breastfeeding cannot be overstated. Your support network might include a variety of people who each bring something valuable to your breastfeeding adventure. Family members and friends who have had their own experiences with breastfeeding can be incredible resources. They can offer practical tips, provide emotional support, and even help with household tasks so you can focus on feeding your baby and resting. Don't overlook the power of professional support as well—lactation consultants, for instance, are invaluable. These experts can offer guidance on everything from latch techniques to solving specific breastfeeding challenges like low milk supply or nipple pain. Healthcare providers, such as your OB/GYN or pediatrician, should also be considered part of this network, ready to offer medical advice and support when needed.

Online Communities

In today's digital age, online forums and social media groups dedicated to breastfeeding can also be a significant part of your support system. These platforms allow you to connect with other breastfeeding parents from around the world, any time of the day or night. Whether you're up for a 3 AM feeding or dealing with a breastfeeding issue, chances are there's someone else online ready to share their experiences or offer some words of encouragement. Websites like La Leche League International, KellyMom, or even specific Facebook groups provide not only community support but also a wealth of information and resources that can help you feel less alone and more empowered. I am currently part of a Facebook group that is for moms over thirty-five years old. I have gotten so much support and information from the group over the years. I highly recommend finding your online communities to supplement your organic support groups of friends and family. My village of friends and family is also invaluable. Collectively we have over 20 children, and we have all had different experiences with breastfeeding and parenting. Their experience and advice is so useful when navigating new situations.

10.2 The Importance of Self-Care: Mental, Emotional, and Physical Health

In the whirlwind of feeding schedules, diaper changes, and sleepless nights, it's easy to place your well-being on the back burner. However, weaving self-care into your daily routine isn't just beneficial; it's necessary to sustain the energy, patience, and joy needed to nurture your little one. Self-care is about carving out moments in your day that replenish your mental, emotional, and physical health, ensuring you're not just surviving, but thriving as a new mom.

Engaging in regular mindfulness practices, such as meditation, can ground your thoughts and reduce anxiety. You can start simply, perhaps with five minutes of focused breathing while your baby naps, or by using guided meditation apps that fit easily into a hectic schedule. Deep-breathing exercises are another quick and effective way to manage stress on the spot. By focusing on your breath, you engage the body's natural relaxation response, which can help temper the chaos of a crying baby or a sleepless night. These practices don't just help you manage stress—they enhance your overall well-being.

Physical activity is another cornerstone of effective self-care. The postpartum period can leave your body feeling different, and often weaker than it was pre-pregnancy. Gentle exercises, such as walking, yoga, or Pilates, can significantly improve your physical health by strengthening muscles, improving circulation, and boosting mood. If finding time alone for exercise sounds like a fairy tale, consider incorporating activities you can do with your baby. For instance, going for a brisk walk with your baby in a stroller or carrier not only gives you the exercise you need but also provides fresh air and a change of scenery for both of you, which can be incredibly refreshing. Yoga classes designed for mothers and babies are also a fantastic way to meet other moms while engaging in physical activity. If you are like me, getting to the gym with three kids is nearly impossible. I have incorporated wall Pilates into my daily morning routine. Sometimes it is only a 2 minute wall plank or bridge, but it is that much. Shameless plug here for the book I wrote while in my most recent postpartum time; Wall Pilates Made Easy by Alexandra Veal.

Let's not forget the importance of nutrition and hydration. Your body needs a steady supply of nutrients to recover from childbirth and to produce nourishing breast milk for your baby. Eating a balanced diet rich in vegetables, fruits, proteins, and whole grains provides the energy necessary to keep up with the demands of new motherhood. Remember, what you eat impacts not just your health, but your baby's too, especially during breastfeeding. Hydration is equally crucial, particularly if you are breastfeeding, as dehydration can reduce your milk supply. Keeping a water bottle within reach, especially where you usually feed your baby, can serve as a constant reminder to drink regularly. This simple practice helps ensure that you stay well-hydrated, supporting both milk production and your overall vitality.

Incorporating these self-care practices into your daily life doesn't require monumental changes; rather, it's about making small adjustments that collectively enhance your well-being. By prioritizing mindfulness, physical activity, and nutrition, you not only foster your health but also model healthy habits for your growing family. Remember, taking care of yourself is not an indulgence—it's a crucial part of being the best mom you can be.

10.3 Personal Time & Celebrating Wins

In the busy world of new motherhood, finding time for yourself can be tough. But it's crucial to remember that taking care of yourself is just as important as caring for your baby. Setting clear boundaries around your personal time helps manage expectations and prevents feeling overwhelmed. Communicate with your partner or family about times when you need to focus on yourself. This might mean having an hour in the evening where someone else takes over baby care so you can relax or do something you enjoy. Efficient time management can help you fit these breaks into your day. Instead of using nap times for chores, use them for self-care activities like reading, exercising, or enjoying a quiet coffee. Make these moments as routine as your baby's feeding schedule. I know it seems impossible, or it did for me. The dishes need doing and the laundry needs folding. Don't even think about the toilet and shower that need to be cleaned. The list of chores you have to do is never-ending, and that is just my point. No matter what you do, there will be dishes; there will be laundry; there will be dirty bathrooms and toys on the floor that need to be picked up. This never-ending list is simply that, so give yourself some grace and take that 15 minutes to do some Pilates or take a walk, call a friend or have a cup of coffee. The chores will always be piling up, no matter what you do, so focus on enjoying life. This is only a phase and your spotless home will be that way again someday, just not today, so do not hold yourself to that standard.

Maintaining hobbies and interests outside of motherhood is key to staying connected with yourself. Continue doing activities you love or explore new ones. This helps keep your mental and emotional health in check and sets a great example for your children about the importance of self-care. Finding time for yourself isn't a luxury—it's necessary for your well-being and helps you be a happier, more balanced parent. Celebrate every level of breastfeeding success, whether it's exclusive breastfeeding, a mix with formula, or occasional breastfeeding. Each step is a testament to your dedication and love, and IT IS ENOUGH.

Acknowledge and celebrate your breastfeeding milestones. Whether it's mastering breastfeeding in public, using a breast pump, or overcoming challenges, recognizing these achievements boosts your confidence and reminds you of your progress. Keeping a journal of these moments can be a great way to track and celebrate your journey. This is one action that I did not commit to, but wish I did. As I am now on my last breastfeeding journey, I wish I had recorded my experiences in more detail to look back on as my children grow.

It's also important to recognize the challenges you've overcome. Each obstacle you face and overcome shows your commitment and resolve. Reflecting on these challenges can strengthen your sense of accomplishment and prepare you for future ones. Sharing your breastfeeding story can inspire and support others. Join support groups, share your experience on blogs or social media, and contribute to a community that uplifts and educates, which is undoubtedly why I have written this book. To share my experiences in hopes that it helps another busy mom like me along her way.

CHAPTER ELEVEN

CONCLUSION

As we draw this guide to a close, I want to take a moment to remind you of why we embarked on this journey together. This book was crafted with a heartfelt mission to provide a comprehensive, evidence-based, yet deeply empathetic guide to breastfeeding for modern moms like you and me. Whether you are just starting out or are looking for ways to enhance your breastfeeding experience, this book has aimed to support, educate, and empower you through every challenge and triumph along the way.

From preparing for breastfeeding in those first precious moments after birth, mastering various latching techniques, to navigating the early challenges of engorgement and sore nipples, we've covered a vast landscape. We delved into the crucial aspects of nutrition and hydration, the dynamics of pumping and storing breast milk, and celebrated the remarkable healing powers of breast milk. Moreover, we emphasized the importance of your self-care and emotional wellness, understanding that the wellbeing of a breastfeeding mom is pivotal to her and her baby's health.

Throughout these pages, I've strived to provide advice and insights without judgment, recognizing that each mom's breastfeeding journey is as unique as her baby. There is no one-size-fits-all approach here, only a wealth of information to help you find your own path. One key to navigating this path is the support network around you. Remember, you're not meant to do this alone. Lean on family, friends, and healthcare professionals. Engage with online communities where you can share, learn, and feel connected to other moms who are experiencing similar joys and challenges as you are. Breastfeeding is a dynamic, evolving process. As your baby grows and changes, so too might your breastfeeding techniques and routines. Stay open to learning and adapting. What works one month may change the next, and that's perfectly okay.

Now, let's talk about you for a moment. Please make your well-being a priority. It's so easy to get caught up in the needs of your little one that you forget about your own. Schedule regular time for yourself, engage in activities that rejuvenate your spirit, and never hesitate to seek help when you need it. Congratulations on your commitment to breastfeeding. Whether you've been at this a few days or several months or are preparing to welcome your little one to the world, every day you breastfeed is a day worth celebrating. Your dedication, love, and effort are building a beautiful foundation for your child's future.

As we part ways in this book, I leave you with a heartfelt message of encouragement. You are doing an incredible job. Remember, you are not alone in this journey. There are countless other moms out there, each with her own story of challenges and triumphs. I encourage you to share your story, too. Whether it's on social media, in support groups, or in quiet conversations with friends, sharing your experience can light the way for others just as they can for you.

Here's to you, to us, and to the journey of breastfeeding—filled with as much love and laughter as it is with challenges and learning. May you continue to find strength, resilience, and immense joy in this beautiful experience. You've got this, and we're all in this together.

Sharing the Journey

Now that you've equipped yourself with all the tools and knowledge for breastfeeding success, it's time to share what you've learned and guide others to find the same support.

By leaving your honest opinion of this book on Amazon, you'll be showing other moms where they can find the information they need and helping them to feel confident in their own breastfeeding journeys.

Thank you for being a part of this. The wisdom and strategies for modern breastfeeding thrive when we share our experiences and insights—and you're helping to keep that tradition alive.

Scan the QR code below to leave a review on Amazon.

REFERENCES:

Skin-to-Skin Contact: How Kangaroo Care Benefits Your ... https://www.healthychildren.org/English/ages-stages/baby/preemie/Pages/About-Skin-to-Skin-Care.aspx

Colostrum: Your Baby's First Meal https://www.healthychildren.org/English/ages-stages/baby/breastfeeding/Pages/Colostrum-Your-Babys-First-Meal.aspx

Feeding on demand: How to read your baby's hunger cues https://www.babycenter.com/baby/breastfeeding/what-is-feeding-on-demand_8822

Top 10 Must-Have Breastfeeding Supplies https://lactationnetwork.com/blog/our-top-10-must-have-breastfeeding-supplies-for-new-moms/

Steps and Signs of a Good Latch - WIC Breastfeeding Support https://wicbreastfeeding.fns.usda.gov/steps-and-signs-good-latch

Breastfeeding Positions, Latch, and Positioning https://llli.org/breastfeeding-info/positioning/

Lactation Consultant: When You Need One & What To Expect https://my.clevelandclinic.org/health/articles/22106-lactation-consultant

Engorgement - WIC Breastfeeding Support - USDA https://wicbreastfeeding.fns.usda.gov/engorgement

Sore Nipples and Breastfeeding: Treatment and Prevention https://www.healthline.com/health/parenting/sore-nipple-breastfeeding

Natural Ways To Boost Milk Supply https://www.forbes.com/health/womens-health/natural-ways-to-boost-milk-supply/

Postpartum Depression | Breastfeeding | CDC https://www.cdc.gov/breastfeeding/breastfeeding-special-circumstances/maternal-or-infant-illnesses/postpartum-depression.html

Meeting Maternal Nutrient Needs During Lactation - NCBI https://www.ncbi.nlm.nih.gov/books/NBK235579/

10 Home Remedies for Mastitis: Cabbage, Essential Oils, ... https://www.healthline.com/health/breastfeeding/home-remedies-for-mastitis

Hydration as a limiting factor in lactation https://pubmed.ncbi.nlm.nih.gov/28561446/

How to Safely and Quickly Lose Weight While Breastfeeding https://www.healthline.com/health/parenting/how-to-lose-weight-while-breastfeeding

Cluster Feeding and Growth Spurts https://wicbreastfeeding.fns.usda.gov/cluster-feeding-and-growth-spurts

Starting your breastfed baby on solid food - ABM https://abm.me.uk/breastfeeding-information/starting-breastfed-baby-onto-solids/

Night weaning and phasing out night feeds: things to think about https://raisingchildren.net.au/babies/sleep/settling-routines/night-weaning

How I Make Tandem Nursing a Toddler and Newborn Work https://www.parents.com/baby/breastfeeding/tips/tandem-nursing-toddler-and-newborn-how-i-make-it-work/

What to Know About Extended Breastfeeding - WebMD https://www.webmd.com/parenting/baby/what-to-know-about-extended-breastfeeding#:~:text=Breastfeeding%20for%2012%20or%20more,%2C%20heart%20disease%2C%20and%20diabetes.

Breastfeeding - World Health Organization (WHO) https://www.who.int/health-topics/breastfeeding#:~:text=Infants%20should%20be%20breastfed%20on,years%20of%20age%20or%20beyond.

Handling criticism about breastfeeding - KellyMom.com https://kellymom.com/ages/older-infant/criticism/#:~:text=Quote%20an%20authority,can%20hear%20it%20for%20themselves.

What is Baby-Led Weaning? Benefits of BLW - Solid Starts https://solidstarts.com/baby-led-weaning/#:~:text=Benefits%20of%20Le

tting%20Your%20Baby%20Self%2DFeed&text=Appetite%20Control%3A%20Baby%20is%20in,reduce%20picky%20eating%20later%20on.

The Best Breast Pumps - The New York Times https://www.nytimes.com/wirecutter/reviews/best-breast-pumps/

Paced Bottle Feeding: How to Do It—and Why You Should! https://www.happiestbaby.com/blogs/baby/paced-bottle-feeding

Breastfeeding and Work: A Balancing Act https://www.un.org/en/un-chronicle/breastfeeding-and-work-balancing-act

Frequently Asked Questions – Pumping Breast Milk at Work https://www.dol.gov/agencies/whd/nursing-mothers/faq

How to handle pumping at work: 5 tips for breastfeeding moms https://utswmed.org/medblog/how-handle-pumping-work-6-tips-breastfeeding-moms/

Breastfeeding preterm born infant: Chance and challenge https://www.ncbi.nlm.nih.gov/pmc/articles/PMC8144854/

Relactation - La Leche League International https://llli.org/breastfeeding-info/relactation/

The Antiviral Properties of Human Milk: A Multitude ... https://www.ncbi.nlm.nih.gov/pmc/articles/PMC7926697/

Breastfeeding and Allergic Diseases: What's New? - PMC https://www.ncbi.nlm.nih.gov/pmc/articles/PMC8145659/

Breastmilk Lotion Recipe and Video Tutorial https://www.newlittlelife.com/2021/02/05/breastmilk-lotion-recipe/

Human Breast Milk: From Food to Active Immune ... https://www.ncbi.nlm.nih.gov/pmc/articles/PMC9016618/

Mindfulness-Based Interventions for Postpartum Depression https://www.ncbi.nlm.nih.gov/pmc/articles/PMC10903316/

23 Effective Time Management Strategies for Moms https://organi zedchaosblog.com/time-management-for-moms/

Exercise after pregnancy: How to get started https://www.mayoclinic.org/healthy-lifestyle/labor-and-delivery/ in-depth/exercise-after-pregnancy/art-20044596

It takes a village: Building your breastfeeding support network https://www.womenshealth.gov/its-only-natural/finding-supp ort/it-takes-village-building-your-breastfeeding-support-network

American Academy of Pediatrics. (2018). Policy statement: Breastfeeding and the use of human milk. *Pediatrics, 142*(6), e20183183. https://doi.org/10.1542/peds.2018-3183

American Academy of Pediatrics. (2021). Sleep-related infant deaths: Updated 2016 recommendations for a safe sleeping environment. *Pediatrics, 138*(5), e20162938. https://doi.org/10.1542/peds. 2016-2938

Grodzinsky, E., & Thang, N. H. (2017). Pacifier use and breastfeeding: A review. *Breastfeeding Medicine, 12*(8), 452-458. https://doi.or g/10.1089/bfm.2017.0111

McDonald, S. J., & Middleton, P. (2016). Pacifiers for term infants after breastfeeding is established. *Cochrane Database of Systematic Reviews, 2016*(9). https://doi.org/10.1002/14651858.CD007202.pub3

Schwarz, J. D. (2020). The effects of pacifier use on infant dental health. *Journal of Pediatric Dentistry, 42*(3), 182-190.

American Academy of Pediatrics. (2012). Breastfeeding and the use of human milk. *Pediatrics, 129*(3), e827-e841. https://doi.org/10.15 42/peds.2011-3552

Victora, C. G., Bahl, R., Barros, A. J. D., França, G. V. A., Horton, S., Krasevec, J., ... & Rollins, N. C. (2016). Breastfeeding in the 21st century:

Epidemiology, mechanisms, and lifelong effect. *The Lancet, 387*(10017), 475-490. https://doi.org/10.1016/S0140-6736(15)01024-7

World Health Organization. (2017). *Protecting, promoting, and supporting breastfeeding in facilities providing maternity and newborn services.*

Mennella, J. A., & Beauchamp, G. K. (1991). Maternal diet alters the sensory qualities of human milk and the nursling's behavior. *Pediatrics, 88*(4), 737-744. https://doi.org/10.1542/peds.88.4.737

Riordan, J., & Wambach, K. (2010). *Breastfeeding and human lactation* (4th ed.). Jones & Bartlett Learning.

World Health Organization. (n.d.). *Breastfeeding and maternal nutrition.*

American Academy of Pediatrics. (n.d.). *Medications and breastfeeding.* Retrieved from

National Institutes of Health. (n.d.). *Drugs and lactation database (LactMed).* Retrieved from

World Health Organization. (n.d.). *Breastfeeding and maternal medication: Recommendations for drugs in the Eleventh WHO Model List of Essential Drugs.* Retrieved from

American Academy of Pediatrics. (n.d.). *Medications and breastfeeding.*

Hale, T. W. (2017). *Medications and mothers' milk 2017.* Springer Publishing Company.

World Health Organization. (n.d.). *Breastfeeding and maternal medications: Recommendations for drugs in the WHO Model List of Essential Drugs.*

www.ingramcontent.com/pod-product-compliance
Lightning Source LLC
Chambersburg PA
CBHW071008120626
46546CB00003B/991